Love the Questions:
University Education and Enlightenment

Semaphore Series

LOVE
THE
QUESTIONS

UNIVERSITY EDUCATION AND ENLIGHTENMENT

Ian Angus

ARP BOOKS • WINNIPEG

Copyright ©2009 Ian Angus

ARP BOOKS (Arbeiter Ring Publishing)
201E-121 Osborne Street
Winnipeg, Manitoba
Canada R3L 1Y4
arpbooks.org

Printed in Canada by Marquis
Cover by Michael Carroll
Second printing, September 2013

MANITOBA ARTS COUNCIL
CONSEIL DES ARTS DU MANITOBA

Canada Council   Conseil des Arts
for the Arts   du Canada

 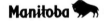

Canadian   Patrimoine
Heritage   canadien

Manitoba

ARP acknowledges the financial support of our publishing activities by Manitoba
Culture, Heritage, and Tourism, and the Government of Canada through the
Canada Book Fund.

ARP acknowledges the support of the Province of Manitoba through the Book
Publishing Tax Credit and the Book Publisher Marketing Assistance Program.

We acknowledge the support of the Canada Council for our publishing program.

With the generous support of the Manitoba Arts Council.

Printed on paper from 100% recycled post-consumer waste.

LIBRARY AND ARCHIVES CANADA CATALOGUING IN PUBLICATION

Angus, Ian H. (Ian Henderson), 1949-
    Love the questions: university education and enlightenment / Ian Angus.

(Semaphore series)
ISBN 978-1-894037-40-2

    1. University autonomy. 2. Academic freedom. 3. Education, Higher—
Aims and objectives. I. Title. II. Series: Semaphore series

LB2322.2.A54 2009   378.1   C2009-902903-0

CONTENTS

For Cassandra
in the hope that she will experience the liberation
that I found through learning and thinking

Emancipate yourselves from mental slavery;
None but ourselves can free our minds.
—Bob Marley, *Redemption Song*

PREFACE

When a student recently asked me for advice on whether to pursue a future in the university, I found that—unlike my previous responses—I could not simply recommend it to him. I realized in that moment that something has irrevocably changed for me. Of course, for many years now I had noticed that many young faculty come into the university in expectation of a cosy middle-class job and very little sense of a vocation, but I was able to dismiss them as careerists who didn't really understand what was going on. I remember how intensely I wanted to teach and write in a university setting when I began as a thinker. I remember how it was bound up with, but not quite the same as, the political commitments that I took on with many others in the 1960s. Being able to think in a university setting was for me continuous with the enlightenment experienced in the sixties when I found a place where the self-satisfied, bland patina of existence available in small-town Ontario was held up to criticism through a higher measure, and expectation, of human life. This book is an attempt to explain what has changed, why now it would not be a bad idea to hedge one's bets on where to pursue critical thinking without letting go of that higher measure. At the same time, I did not want to write another lament about the fate of the university. For one thing, the university remains a place where much real learning and teaching—yes, enlightenment—takes place. For another, it is not simply a matter of fate. Real decisions and events have still to take place that might change the picture in important ways. So, I have tried to balance a realistic assessment of the state of the contemporary university and the forces that would undermine it with a sense of what can be saved, reinvented, or discovered of its potential. I have also written not of a single university, or of a provincial or national policy—though no doubt my reflections are rooted in my experience in Canada and my seven years teaching in the United States. The university is an "idea" deeply rooted in the European sense of the essence of human being as a striving to understand its place in the whole. There is a long-established genre of writing about this idea. I wanted to take the idea seriously without setting aside the realistic assessment. It has been useful for me to think over the commitments that have driven my life as a professor and that seem to me uniquely endangered today. It is characteristic of the humanities, at least as I understand them, that preservation of the intellectual heritage and the courage to understand what is new are tightly woven together. I hope that these reflections may be of use to others as they grapple with their futures in and around the only institution that is constitutively committed to enlightenment. In writing, though I have attempted to lighten the often over-burdened academic style, I found it necessary to rely on two concepts: "enlightenment" for the philosophical heritage, which takes the measure of factual situations, and "techno-science" for analysis of the situation of the facts. I have included two notes separate from the main text on the genesis and meaning of these concepts and made reference to these notes only at the first use of the concept.

I would like to thank Sean Rupka for his extensive bibliographic research and Peter Ives and Arbeiter Ring Publishing for once again making publishing an experience of a shared project. Their enthusiasm for this book has meant a lot to me. The two prior readers of the text provided invaluable commentary and criticism.

CHAPTER 1

WHAT IS THE UNIVERSITY?

Who should care about the future of the university? Why should they care? The university used to be an elite institution that most working people rarely encountered. The training and socialization that the elite classes received prior to taking up leading positions in government and industry was arguably as much of a right of passage as a search for enlightenment. Of course there were always those few for whom the love of knowledge and the reading of great texts was a consuming passion. But if one were concerned only with those people, there would be few larger social issues to be raised about the university in society.

The situation is different now. In the United States and Canada about a quarter of the working population has completed a university degree. In 2001, 76% of Canadians in the twenty to twenty-two-year-old age bracket had some post-secondary education. While 10% of the baby boom generation attended university, now about 40% do so. These figures put Canada fourth internationally, behind the United States, Norway and the Netherlands. (References for specific figures cited, quotations and general sources have been collected in a section at the back of the book called "References and Further Reading" that is organized on a chapter-by-chapter basis.) But beyond comparisons, the more important fact is that increasing attendance in higher education is an international trend that is deeply rooted in economic and technological changes. Even more important, it is a trend that is not likely to reverse and countries that do not keep up will be confined to marginal status. It has been said that we live in a knowledge society and there is no doubt that contemporary society is deeply committed to the extension of knowledge and its rapid utilization in innovations. This is true not only of scientific and technical knowledge but also of social scientific and even humanistic pursuits to the extent that they can be oriented to the market. To this extent the future of the university should provoke widespread social concern. Add to this the fact that the university has in recent years changed to such a degree that it hardly resembles what previous generations experienced under that name.

The corporate university has been waging a battle for some years now against the remaining features of the public university. The major means of this battle has been fiscal. In the same way that right-wing governments at the provincial and national levels began their restructuring with the claim that there was not, or no longer, sufficient money to sustain current social insurance/welfare practices, university administrations have justified their restructuring with the claim that governments are no longer willing to support the public university and that they have no other option but to seek funding from other sources. This is by no means an empty claim. Public funding of universities has consistently fallen for decades now and major issues about the functioning and purposes of the university need to be addressed. This fall in government funding has gone hand-in-hand with seeing education as simply an aid to the individual in confronting the job market, so that any larger social or public purposes lose their purchase. University administrations, on the whole, have avoided addressing larger questions of the social role of education or the current restructuring of the university directly because of their bureaucratic, rather than political, approach to university functioning. They have presented the new fiscal environment as an inescapable force that has inevitably turned them toward corporate sources of funding. Whereas government block funding left the universities more or less free to determine the use of funds internally, corporate funding is usually targeted toward specific purposes of which it approves. Government funding has now begun to mimic this dedication of funds to external purposes. In an era of dedicated funding, grant money, and distance education money grabs, the university is no longer a unity that can define its own priorities. Funding of specific functions prevails and the whole becomes simply the sum of its dominant parts. Increased corporate funding has supported some aspects of the university at the expense of others and ultimately transformed the public university into the corporate university with barely a word of debate. Mainly, this has been done without dismantling procedures and practices directly but by simply voiding them of real content. Debates are cut off with reference to fiscal Realpolitik and the priorities of the Dean or higher administration. The corporate university has thus come into being in concert with the undermining of democratic decision making in the university and a rise in the power of administrations responsible only to government and corporate sources of funding—not to the internal core of the university based in the educative experience. Suppressing of genuine debate about the function of the university and its social role has been key to this transformation. While fiscal abandonment by a waning welfare state and the rise of new information technologies are certainly a reality, the absolute necessity of a corporate transformation is not. The absence of debate on this crucial fact has spread throughout the corporate university like a virus: we are now confronted with discourses of necessity and decline on all fronts. But this helplessness is a product, not a fact, and it can be contested. The tail is now wagging the dog: administrations and administrators run the university; there seems to be no alternative to corporate funding—which means corporate priorities—and the university's critical function has become vestigial. Those who keep it alive are used as window dressing to prevent others from seeing what's going on.

One begins to suspect that the current state of the university is an important place where the destiny of knowledge, and self-knowledge—that is our heritage from the past, and our duty to recreate in the present—is being put to a severe test.

How does one define the university? It serves many functions (economic, political, ideological, etc.) and undertakes many activities (research, instruction, technical innovation, etc.). In today's climate it is tempting to define the university "materialistically" as a private-public partnership, or corporate-state joint economic institution, producing training and credentials (and therefore defining others who do not attend or fail as untrained and without credentials) recognized in the global corporate economy or the national bureaucracy. This is not wrong. Indeed it is the reality of the contemporary corporate university that those who work and learn within it must address it in some fashion or another. For many, it is simply the environment within which they go about their daily business and thus as natural and unquestionable as any other. But given the still relatively recent transformation of the public university into a corporate environment, and given the still incomplete nature of this transformation, a memory of other practices and legitimations survives. During the era of the welfare state, the government-funded university was understood to play a public role in developing citizenship and social awareness that shaped and over-rode its economic function. This memory serves to make many others uncomfortable with the new corporate reality of the university. University culture is now torn between the memory of better days that leads to a narrative of decline and despair and a new "realistic" resignation to the "fact" that the university is simply an economic institution no different from any other, except insofar as making shoes is different from renting high-rises.

There was always a minority for whom the corporate function, and even the previous citizenship function of the public, state-supported university, were questionable as such. After the Second World War, the university continued the function of social criticism that has always hung around those who ask basic questions about human being and social organization. The socially critical activities of individual faculty were more or less tolerated in the 1960s, but when faculty and students tried to align the university as an institution with democratic forces outside in opposition to the government-corporation nexus, the possibility was soon closed down. Often the police were invoked to keep the university within its established function, for example at the London School of Economics, Simon Fraser University in British Columbia, and in the almost classical case of the Free Speech Movement at the University of California at Berkeley. A critical minority was more acceptable within the public university than it is within the corporate one, though there were always limits. Thus, there is now a tendency for radical critics to succumb to the liberal and social democratic narrative of decline, forgetting that the public role of the university in the welfare state was an interlude in a longer history in which university education was a key ideological and practical preparation for a career in the imperial adventure. The British Empire — or French, German, etc. — needed administrators and bureaucrats as much as soldiers, informants and head-breakers. The Canadian state continued to play this role within its own borders. The public university was itself a transformation of the traditional role of the elite university.

Such a materialistic definition provokes discomfort in those of us who work and study in the university. Not because it is wrong but because it is right. Nevertheless, it fails to capture that for which we struggle when we teach and learn — the ability to think meaningfully about one's experience that allows a deeper judgment of the current situation and brings one's future actions into question — what one can still call "enlightenment." The struggle for enlightenment in its individual, social, technical and biological dimensions has never by any means been limited to the university, but the dignity of the university's role has rested on its claim to a link with the project of enlightenment. It is this claim that unsettles the purely materialistic definition of the university. Thus the "idealistic" definition that the university is "a community of scholars" resurges when one attempts to articulate the project that animates learning. It is all too easy to document the failures that prove that this definition does not capture the everyday practice of university life. It is more difficult to abandon it entirely in the face of an inquiring student or one's own struggle to confront despair or madness.

The university is an institution of thought. Thus, its economic and political functions are pervaded by a practice whose distinctiveness consists in its attempt to transcend those functions by inquiring into their justification and their place in the wider social order. The university has been most itself when it has approximated in practice this struggle for enlightenment. Must this definition remain "idealistic," that is to say, must it ignore the realities of economy and politics? Is it only an ideology that dissimulates? It would seem so if the struggle for enlightenment were severed from its practical base in the encounter that produces education. However, even the most mundane practices of the university, such as curriculum committee meetings, hiring decisions or rules about plagiarism, involve references to the moral and social significance of education. While such legitimation contains a perennial slide toward becoming a comforting ideology that merely masks a rude reality, it can never become entirely so due to the specificity of education as a practice. It is this specificity that accounts for the fact that there was always a minority for whom the corporate function, and even the citizenship function, were questionable as such. Thus, in this sense the critics are well-placed. Their criticism is rooted in a practice that cannot be entirely dissipated as long as any distinction remains between education and selling shoes. This unerasable claim to enlightenment is what has been classically called the "idea" of the university. Even today, the institution cannot function without its claim to embody the idea.

The practical and organizational core of the institution of thought is the seminar room with its interchange between younger, beginning thinkers and one or more older, experienced ones. This encounter is not an exchange of information (which produces nothing new) but precisely an *encounter*, an event. The event of embodied reflection animates the struggle for enlightenment. It is no wonder that the corporate university in the most wealthy countries in the world cannot find sufficient resources to fund encounters in seminar rooms. While the public university of the welfare state was more accommodating, it also contained a tendency toward imparting information to serve purposes decided elsewhere. Both citizenship and corporate models prefer the lecture hall with its many listeners and few experts to the common struggle of the seminar room. Lectures can be learned and witty. They can be benign, taken in moderation, but the core of the university is the search for a not-yet-discovered understanding, a still-elusive formulation. This search produces enlightenment, not the supposed possession of knowledge itself that could be transmitted to the largest possible number of adherents. To define the university in this manner is not necessarily "idealistic" in the sense of ignoring the material realities that make the university possible and invade its practices. It is simply a definition through the best of what the university does, based in a specific activity that the university did not create but to which it has given form, which concretizes enlightenment as the most fundamental and universal human task.

The core of the university is the encounter between students and faculty and it is their responsibility to undertake that encounter in a spirit of enlightenment. Otherwise, what they do could be done better elsewhere. A community engaged in the search for knowledge enacts critical thinking. Relationships between students and between faculty are also transformed by the seminar into experiences of co-questioning. In the absence of the co-questioning encounter, these relationships tend to degenerate into competition or mutual indifference. It is significant that it is hard to get students to participate in a seminar nowadays; they seem to think that it is a fraud because the professor already has the answer. But this is a myth; it is not learning that justifies teaching, but the ability to ask and confront genuine questions. The idea of the university can be defined as loving the questions.

The justification for academic freedom is in the activity of critical thinking. Genuine searching requires criticism of received truth and constituted powers, and demands the mutual criticism of students and teachers based in the quality of their ideas rather than their social positions. Criticism is of the idea, not the person, and is not only compatible with mutual respect of persons but demands and reinforces such respect. Despite its embodiment in the seminar room, this activity cannot be confined to the university. It has a wider importance that provokes a critique of all those forces which prevent enlightenment and which entrench domination and ignorance. Occasionally, thinkers who have taken this project seriously have been drawn to articulate in the public realm as social criticism the ethic that is built into the practice of university teaching and learning. For this, they have often been stigmatized by the powerful in university and society as "outspoken academics" wandering outside their supposed academic specialties without understanding, or even repressing, the ethic that is embodied within all such inquiries, specialist or otherwise. The socially relevant critical thinker has no guarantee of truth—any more than any other human—but the corrective for this is in an expanded sphere of critical thinking, not in its curtailment. One must ask who is really outspoken in the society in which we live. Corporations, government, and the media say long and loud what they have to say. They shout from all corners and are impossible to avoid in today's propagandistic consumer environment. When these powers stigmatize an academic for being outspoken, the intent should be clear. It is to keep public awareness and debate from extending to these powers and their social role itself. University-based thinkers are not the only ones to raise such issues but they are one crucial source for social criticism. Another important source, which also often stimulates research questions for academics, is

contemporary social movements such as environmental-
ism, feminism, trade unionism, anti-racist movements,
city reform movements, and so forth. Some of the best
university-based research in recent years has been when
independent scholars have investigated the social issues
addressed by social movements and addressed their results
to the wider public. It is a powerful combination that produces thoughtful material for public reflection.

I said that the current state of the university raises
the question of the destiny of self-knowledge. But this is
important not only for those who are within the university. The public role of the university is to safeguard the
struggle for self-knowledge throughout society. And this
public role can only be properly exercised if citizens and
social actors take an interest in the role of the university.

CHAPTER II

EDUCATION AS ENLIGHTENMENT

I want to begin my reflections on the current state of the university with an experience of teaching, since it is this encounter that most directly encompasses what is important and unique about the university. When a seminar works well it brings the assumptions of both teacher and students into view and holds them up for critical examination. To a large extent, the critical examination that I am undertaking in this little book is a result of beginning to see clearly and think through my assumption that education is enlightenment (see the note on enlightenment after the main text). I want to begin by illustrating the process.

A STORY ABOUT TEACHING

In the summer term of 2002, I was teaching a second year course that I had taught several times — Humanities

202: Great Texts in the Humanities II—which covers the period between the seventeenth century and the present. According to the calendar description, the course is oriented to "an intensive study of some of the major works which have had a formative influence on the structure and development of western thought" and proceeds through "reading and discussion of primary texts and the major themes which emerge from them" in order to "introduce students to the essential philosophical, literary, social and religious themes of western civilization." Given that this is a thirteen-week course, such a description might give any instructor grounds for despair. It reads more like an outline for a life's study than an introduction to anything at all. No doubt many of my fellow college and university teachers have had this experience. Designing the course is rather a challenge.

If one adds to this intrinsic impossibility of success the practical constraint that the texts chosen have to be readable in one or, at most, two weeks and comprehensible to second year undergraduates with no specific background, it is no surprise that the course has become known colloquially as "great *short* texts." It is certainly my experience that only short texts can be discussed in sufficient detail and quantity to give any sense of the development of modern thought over this period. One must, above all, serve to illustrate that great texts cannot be digested in large gulps or disposed of by waves of the hand. In my view, one also has to choose a theme that one can follow through many, if not all, of the texts so that the course has a unity and does indeed give some sense of *development*. I have chosen science and technology, tradition and enlightenment, and well as various other themes. Luckily one does not always have to select entirely different texts when one alters the thematic focus. René Descartes' *Discourse on Method* makes it onto almost all my lists.

That particular summer I wanted to trace the emergence of the modern notion of the individual alongside the tendency to giganticism that one finds in modernity in order to provoke students to think about our knee-jerk ethical individualism that takes place in the middle of massive social organization and conformity—indeed, to think this co-existence as a single problem. My list included Etienne de la Boétie, *Discourse on Voluntary Servitude*; René Descartes, *Discourse on Method*; John Locke, *A Letter Concerning Toleration*; Mary Shelley, *Frankenstein, or the Modern Prometheus*; Karl Marx and Friedrich Engels, *The Communist Manifesto*; Sigmund Freud, *The Future of an Illusion*; Rainer Maria Rilke, *Letters to a Young Poet*; George Orwell, *Burmese Days*; and Oscar Wilde, *The Soul of Man*. Locke, Orwell and Wilde were also new to this version of the course, but it was Rilke who thrust me into a controversy that I haven't resolved yet.

Rilke's *Letters* contain discussions of many issues of moment—death, love, nature, solitude, writing, poverty—in which one can lose oneself in a pub, a coffee shop, or even a classroom. These discussions are animated by a passionate and unconditional commitment to an ideal of self-expression that has come to be known as the romantic ideal. The term is all right for historical reasons, as long as it doesn't become an excuse for throwing it on the rubbish heap. My students made immediate use of this heap, though without using the term as their excuse. (I should say parenthetically that in speaking of "my students" in this book I am referring to the majority sentiment as expressed at the time. Speaking this way does justice neither to individuals, unexpressed views, afterthoughts, nor the longer-term effects of teaching, though it is necessary to express the difference in expectations from reading that I am writing about now.) Rilke argued that "the creator must be a world for himself and find everything in himself and in Nature to whom he has attached himself" (p. 21). He urged the would-be writer to search for the reason for this aspiration and would only accept the answer "I must" in contrast to all outward reckoning (pp. 18–9). He added that "works of art are of an infinite loneliness" (p. 29) suggesting that Franz Kappus (to whom the letters were addressed) "try to love the *questions themselves* like locked rooms and like books that are written in a very foreign tongue" (p. 35). At the bottom of this commitment is a decision to "assume our existence as *broadly* as we in any way can; everything, even the unheard of, must be possible in it" (p. 67). The romantic ideal is instituted by a *decision* to assume one's own experience as the starting point for the activity of writing poetry. This decision is even more important than the writing of poetry itself. It is what makes writing poetry possible. Even more important, it is what poetry itself seeks to awaken and instil. "Art too is only a way of living," says Rilke on the last page.

I was interested in this ideal as a way of making sense of the experience of creating and being affected by art, especially modern art—indeed, of the ubiquity of the idea of "creation" itself. But I was even more interested in the contribution of this originally artistic ideal to the living of life in the modern world, its contribution to the critique of ordinary life, of "ordinariness" as such, and the continuous broadening and generalization of the ideal of self-expression to ever-larger spheres of life. I discussed the effect of this ideal on love and marriage, friendship, and work. I wanted to show how self-expression and self-development was a vital modern moral practice. I wanted to show why many of the great modern poets and philosophers—Nietzsche, Freud, Marx, Baudelaire, Wilde, and Rilke himself—saw nothing more important than this great struggle, nothing to which it could be secondary, risking and suffering poverty, ostracism, madness, and death in its name. I had to summon all my rhetorical powers, because I realized that I was not carrying my audience with me.

The simple truth is that although they understood what I was saying, and they understood that Rilke expressed something about a way of living profoundly immersed in modernity, they simply could not summon up any positive feeling about it. They felt no attraction to it. I was reduced to asking them to hold their criticism for a moment and find something good to say about it. Their answers were uncharacteristically ordinary and uninspiring. They understood but it just didn't seem to touch them. I must admit to being horrified.

This was a very unusual teaching experience for me. That is why I'm still thinking about it years later. There have been precedents, of course. I taught a course in the United States on utopias during the 1980s because the student mood was so disillusioned in comparison with my own student days. But they gradually garnered some enthusiasm for utopia even if it couldn't be realized. Indeed, the idea of utopia is that it can't be realized. I even managed to design a little technique for producing a utopia, so that each student could write one. I received an essay from a black woman student about a world without racism that brought tears to my eyes. In the case of Rilke, however, I have never so thoroughly felt that my own commitments and those of the students to whom I was talking had greatly diverged.

This event has remained a *topos* for reflection, a place to which I return. It is a reflection on my own origins, both the depth and the spontaneity of my commitment to self-expression: How did it come to be that an eighteen-year old from a small town in southern Ontario had already become passionately attached to this moral ideal? I remember saying at that time in the late 1960s that everyone has at least one great novel or poem in them struggling to come out. Never mind whether that naïve statement is right. By what means of cultural transmission and reinvention had that ideal come to grip me? I'm still asking that question. Also, how can these students do without it? Or, do they really do without it? Is it just reticence, the fear of speaking their commitments, or the fear of commitment itself, which holds them back? There is something in this but it is not the whole answer. What does it mean to live a life not dedicated to self-expression? Is a life without self-expression worth living? The social scientific banality that we are all "socialized" to belong in our family, group, class and society gives an easy excuse for not asking these questions. Looking back to my own origins, I tried to understand and explain the experience of my students: attempting a dialogue, an experiment in understanding, that itself would need to bridge the years between 1968 and the early twenty-first century, probe the limits of "socialization," and, finally, make me confront my own unspoken commitment to self-expression as enlightenment.

Later that term we read the *Manifesto of the Communist Party*. A significant number reacted to the critique of capitalism with approbation. In Marx and Engels the critique of capitalism is intrinsically connected to the method of its overthrow: capitalism concentrates and organizes the workers in order to exploit labour more thoroughly. The newly organized workers experience their labour as the creation of the world in which they live. They are no longer the passive artifacts of their past formation. Thus, "workers of the world unite." The new world free of exploitation is already visible in the critique of capitalism. Students divided this analysis into its two constituent parts: the critique of capitalism they assessed as having some merit (worth discussing anyway), but the classless society was immediately relegated to being an unrealizable ideal not worth much breath. This bifurcation of the two elements, whose connection is the specific claim of Marxism to uniqueness, is not a bad starting point for learning. One can point out that it is the connection that is key to Marxism as such. One can show that, if the prospective classless society is not a viable ideal, then the critique of contemporary capitalism cannot be accepted in the terms in which it has been presented. One can point out that any future-oriented ideal may perhaps never be actualizable as such. One can show how the historical experience of Communism discredits certain readings of Marx but leaves open other less-acknowledged possibilities.

In other words, despite the tendency nowadays to treat Marx as a dead dog, the pertinence of his critique of capitalism to contemporary neo-liberal globalization keeps the discussion interesting and takes it to new levels in which one's thinking must be sharpened and go beyond the formulations of the text itself. What more could one want from a great short text aiming to introduce students to essential themes of western civilization? What keeps the discussion of Marx going is his critical realism that is presented in seamless unity with the romantic ideal. What is taken to be unrealistic utopianism in Marx is precisely the ideal of self-expression to which Rilke gave potent voice. But the critique depends upon the ideal and upon the ideal becoming a moral practice. Otherwise the critique becomes "purely theoretical" and doesn't cut it in the world of work and social institutions. Critique without crisis is a purely theoretical enterprise. By "crisis" I mean a situation in the lived world that presents alternative possibilities that demand to be addressed in action. I don't conclude from this, as many of my students might, that it is thereby without value, but its social significance is drastically reduced thereby. There is no crisis if self-expression as a moral practice is rejected because the frustration of self-expression does not provoke a critique oriented to change. The future tense is lost. The present extends indefinitely into the future without break. Crisis is the presently experienced possibility of a break, and the romantic ideal is the determination to live this crisis thoroughly and without reservation, to take our existence upon ourselves as broadly as we can.

This is why I find my students' out-of-hand dismissal of Rilke's ideal as expressed in the context of poetry more significant for contemporary demoralization than their ability to accept parts of Marx. Rilke is more one-sided, more focussed, in this sense. His purpose is exclusively to explain the decision for self-expression that underlies poetry and to explain that this decision permeates one's whole life, whether one writes poetry or not. That exclusivity underlines the radicality of the decision for self-expression. It is this radicality whose reception is clouded by the duality that the contemporary eye sees in Marx and whose clarity in Rilke brings forth only a stunned silence. The students were more sympathetic to

Franz Kappus himself, who explained in the introduction to Rilke's letters that "life drove me off into those very regions from which the poet's warm, tender and touching concern had sought to keep me" (p. 13). Kappus concluded that the strenuous romantic ideal was only for a favoured few. Of the subsequent turn of his own life he remarks, "but that is not important" and adds that "where a great and unique man speaks, small men should keep silence" (p. 13). It is not often that one of the sheep articulates the Nietzschean solution that some are great lions and others are sheep. I have always thought that the most basic task of a teacher is to fight Kappus' resignation, to provoke every student to refuse to say of his or her own life "that is not important" whether they are great or not — indeed, to question this false standard of greatness. This basic task is what connects teaching to social enlightenment. Taking any measure whatever, not all will measure up, but, wherever each one may be, a further step toward self-knowledge is possible.

One could divide the human species between those who are capable of self-expression and those who are not. One can cede history to the great men, and now women too. One can cede education too, of course. This is the most likely alternative in our supposedly democratic university. Or one could, as my students seem to have done, dump it altogether for the practicality of training. And then where would we be? Must I be either an elitist or a democratic sheep? Is this the only option? Is it not possible in this time to be committed to self-expression for everyone, to enlightenment? It is in this question that the dialogue between me and my students, between 1968 and the twenty-first century, begins. That is where the journey that has led to this book began.

WHAT IS ENLIGHTENMENT?

The contemporary university is thus both a PPP (public-private partnership), like hospitals, transportation, and many other services that used to be exclusively state-sponsored, and the place where a heritage of critical thought belongs. Bringing the heritage of critical thought to bear on contemporary institutions is precisely what I mean by enlightenment. Enlightenment is an *intervention* into the present situation that draws on the resources of the past for inspiration and guidance. This intervention has its own effects: one is to open up new interpretations of the heritage — which makes the past come alive and retain its significance; another is to create new thinking in the present — which adds to the heritage that future generations can draw upon.

In recent years, there have been many critics of enlightenment. Most, if not all, are really referring to the period of the eighteenth century called the Enlightenment (with a capital E). This period gave us the idea of progress through the application of science and technology to social problems. There are many reasons why the idea of progress, especially understood in this way, is not a viable way to address contemporary issues. However, this does not mean that the concept of enlightenment is itself bankrupt. First of all, the Enlightenment was called by that name because it approximated the idea of enlightenment that preceded it, not the other way around. The concept of enlightenment goes back to Socrates (at least) who asked about the meaning of concepts like justice, piety, courage, and friendship in ancient Greece (fifth century B.C.). In order to subject these concepts to critical analysis neither he nor his interlocutors could simply assume that their traditional meanings were adequate. In fact, it is the loosening of belief in the traditional meaning of these concepts (which I called "crisis" above) that motivates Socrates' questioning. The questioning itself includes both "critique," which shows the inadequacy of the traditional meanings proffered, and the proposal of an alternative that better addresses current issues. So our current task is not to throw out the concept of enlightenment, but to criticize its inadequate forms and to invent a new form of enlightenment adequate to our tasks.

The modern understanding of enlightenment is especially indebted to Immanuel Kant and his little essay entitled "What is Enlightenment?" (1784). Kant lived in the time of the French Revolution and he accepted the important task of his time to understand this revolution and its role in the history of humanity. His starting point was the well-known observation that everyone makes mistakes. Authoritarian bodies of all sorts use this fact to reject the possibility of people thinking for themselves. In so doing, they assume, or even perhaps believe, that those in authority make fewer mistakes, especially since the majority have no training in making important decisions. Politicians of all stripes make use of this argument nowadays when they claim that they should be re-elected because they have greater experience. Existing powers always have this advantage. Kant pointed out that, under conditions of authority, one does not learn from one's mistakes because one can always blame one's error on the authority. Under conditions of freedom, however, one has to accept responsibility for one's mistakes, change one's thinking and activity, and get closer to the truth. Thus, Kant argued that "the public use of one's reason must always be free" though he accepted that certain "private" uses of reason can be subject to authority. He had in mind primarily the subjection of the clergy to church doctrine in giving their sermons. At that time, the task was to introduce into society a realm in which there could be free discussion. Naturally, at first, this had to be a limited and special space but over time it could be expanded. Many organizations that the eighteenth century would have seen as private are better now regarded as public. Corporations, for example, make decisions with environmental consequences that they regard as private decisions, while many citizens think that, because they are affected by those decisions, they should be regarded as public. The shifting line between public and private is one of those changes through which the Kantian model of enlightenment can be brought up to date. Kant's understanding of enlightenment focuses on the public effect of critique and rests upon the prior courage of the one who dares to think for him or herself—like Socrates, for example.

The twentieth century phenomenological concept of critique takes its departure from the recognition that established institutions affect not only the way that we act but also the way that we think. They contain the possibility of shutting down alternatives to the present way of doing things by preventing the right questions from emerging. A phenomenological critique traces an institution back to its "instituting" moment, not its historical emergence as such but the basic reformation of experience through which the institution comes to be. That basic reformation creates a before/after temporal structure which marks our historical situation and, perhaps, limit. To be born after the introduction of compulsory public schooling rather than before, for example, means not only that one will have to go to school but that one will tend to think of education solely in terms of schools. If one can understand sufficiently well the "constitutive assumptions" of an institution then one can push back this limit. More options for action then become available. Critique of institutions in this sense is a form of public critique that addresses the formation of our thoughts and assumptions by powerful institutions.

Both Kant and phenomenological thinkers have operated mainly within the modern university, unlike Socrates and Greek philosophy generally. I mean the discussions of university teaching and "enlightenment" thus far to have given some indication of why they are tied up together. It is the task of the next chapter to explain why the modern university is intrinsically committed to enlightenment. It is this commitment to enlightenment that is endangered by the corporatization of the university.

CHAPTER III

THE UNIVERSITY IN HISTORY

The university is in crisis. It should be clear by now that everything that I am going to say about the university has a moral, evaluative element. I will try to justify this evaluative basis not in general terms but in terms specific to the rise and development of the university as an institution. The source of current anxiety is that, defined in the terms that gave it being and life, the university may have come to an end. To understand this situation we have to look back at what made the university the particular kind of institution that it has been.

Many discussions of the contemporary university try to isolate the *idea* of the university and then analyze and criticize its structure with this measuring rod. We will see this way of thinking in action in Wilhelm von Humboldt's and Cardinal Newman's classical discussions of the university. This approach may have made sense when one was designing and constructing university in the first place (Humboldt) or when there was a clear continuity in the function of the university (Newman). One would have had to have some idea of what one was designing and what purpose it was to fulfil; one would have to know what one was doing within an uninterrupted tradition. However, it would be a mistake to analyze the contemporary university in that way. It would produce a truncated measuring rod and it would be all too simple, like all conservative critiques, to show that the university is *no longer* what it *ought* to be, that is to say, what is used to be, or, rather, what we imagine that it used to be. But the contemporary university is a composite of several different traditions that have themselves been altered considerably in relation to ongoing challenges. It would also be a mistake, however, to throw out the necessity for a measuring rod altogether and capitulate to mere description—which would accept the inevitability of contemporary developments continuing into the future. Though it is useful to know how the contemporary university actually works, it leads us nowhere unless we can evaluate, or *measure*, these workings and, to take their measure, we must have some *ought* in our language. In order to articulate a critique we must deploy a moral language. My solution is this: looking back at history we can discern three different traditions that have affected the university; looking at the contemporary situation we can describe the changes in these traditions and the tendencies that seek to undermine them; thus, looking ahead, we can sketch, at least in outline, what might be possible for a university in the future. In this way, the ethical basis for critique can be found in the history of the university itself and not merely superimposed arbitrarily upon it.

THE MODERN UNIVERSITY

The modern university is the most recent in a long history of institutions designed to facilitate learning. The ancient Greek world produced a number of philosophical and scientific schools that created their own organizations. The Pythagoreans were a mystically inclined mathematical society. The philosopher Plato formed his own Academy, from which we get the term "academic," as did other philosophers such as Aristotle. Such schools pursued knowledge in the spirit of their founder, though they often went through a number of changes and lasted several hundred years. It was a matter of choice which one to attend and many later philosophers attended more than one famous school. They had a public role but they were not supported by the city-state and were not expected to be impartial.

The theological world view of the Middle Ages gave rise to the medieval university, which was built upon the monkish ideal of contemplation. The early modern university trained an aristocratic and administrative elite for the emerging nation-state. We can conclude that every society designs a learning institution in its own image for the production and transmission of knowledge. This learning institution both reflects the form of society and yet, in the best instance, gains a certain distance from it. It is perhaps better to say that the learning institution reflects the *ideal* of the society where what the society believes in, and aspires to, is articulated and transmitted. So while the university is a social institution, it is a very special one that does not only mirror the society but also seeks to *know* the goals and purpose of that society. The Greek schools sought a form of knowledge that the individual could use in distinguishing himself in front of gods and men. The medieval university sought to know the belief (be it Christian, Jewish or Muslim) on which the society was founded. The modern university begins with the concept of reason.

Modern society is committed to a certain concept of reason that completes itself in technological applications. This is easy enough to see in our present world even though it took several hundred years to come into its own. The first modern university to be founded was the University of Berlin, which was funded by the King and where lectures first began in 1810. Wilhelm von

Humboldt was in charge of the Prussian educational system at the time. His idea of the university was based on the importance of self-knowledge for human life. This is a classical ideal that would encompass the Greek schools and the medieval university as well. The significantly modern part of Humboldt's ideal of self-knowledge can be seen in his idea of the university institution as a place where "learning in the widest sense of the word may be cultivated, and where the contents of learning, produced not with the intention of serving education, but being naturally best suited for it, may be given over to the nation's mental and moral education." The German term here translated as learning is *Wissenschaft*, which means science in the broadest sense that would include what the French call "human sciences," and the Germans "spiritual sciences" (*Geisteswissenschaften*) such as the study of literature, history and politics as well as natural sciences. By that time, science had already been specialized into different domains so that, as Humboldt said, "the realm of science is so immense that it can be worked over in its most diverse parts and each part by the most diverse methods." Thus, the problem of how these diverse sciences can come together into a unity of self-knowledge is already there at the founding of the modern university. The further claim that the self-knowledge produced by science is pertinent to the education of *citizens* is also already there.

The modern university is founded on the idea of self-knowledge in a particular form that demands a unity of the sciences and a relation to citizenship and thereby the nation-state. This complex of ideas that emerged in the founding of the University of Berlin came to influence all other universities in modern society, not only those founded later. The founding of the University of London in 1826 broke the Church's monopoly on higher education in Britain and incorporated the idea—propagated by Sydney Smith, Adam Smith, Jeremy Bentham and others—that learning should have a practical utility. This new ideal also came to transform those universities that had been founded earlier and influenced by the monastic or Greek ideal so that all modern universities have come to take over this legacy.

The modern university sits in a crucial place in modern society. It is funded by the nation-state and expected to contribute to citizenship. It is focussed on reason that is both divided into specialized domains of knowledge and yet expected to be unified in the form of self-knowledge. Since modern specialized knowledge produces technical applications, it would not be long until the other main modern institution—the capitalist economy—came into the picture. Because of their influence on government and their desire to market technical applications, allied with their distrust of the ideal of self-knowledge and desire for trained personnel, corporations came to take an interest in the university.

It is of course a very long story how the university with which we are familiar over the last few decades came into being and took the form that it takes today. It is also a story that has taken a somewhat different form in different countries. But I am not trying to tell that story in detail here. I am trying to show the logic of the modern university—how its initial constitution opened up an evolution that has led us to where we are today. The modern university stands between the nation-state and the capitalist economy, between the ideal of citizenship and marketable applications. This social location is centred on the university's main purpose: reason. The focus on reason is the basis for the historical continuity of the modern university with the earlier medieval and Greek forms. However, the form of reason changed in the modern period. A new mathematical science came into being with Galileo and Descartes, a science whose inbuilt tendency to technical applications was already emphasized by Bacon and Descartes. This particular modern form of reason tied the university to a combination of science and technology that contained internal tensions. Basically, the problem was division and unity. Increasing specialization of science led to an increasing difficulty to maintain that science was unified in self-knowledge. But if this ideal can no longer be maintained, the connection of the university to citizenship becomes more tenuous, as does its connection to the older, classical ideal based in the Greek schools that self-knowledge was what one needed to live well.

LIBERAL EDUCATION

The story of the University of Berlin allows us to isolate one major aspect of the modern university due to the predominance of the modern concept of reason. But this is not the only source of the contemporary university. Another main strand is rooted in its continuity with the medieval and classical ideal of self-knowledge as what is most needful for human life. In its medieval and Christian form this ideal is interpreted to mean that self-knowledge is knowledge of one's dependence on God. The prior Greek, and also Roman, "pagan" heritage is devoid of the Christian God, of course, and claims rather that human reason can by itself know the Good well enough to orient human life without any higher source. This continuous tradition of Western humanism influenced the teaching of the humanities in the university curriculum and, to this day, inspires it.

The classic text in the English-speaking tradition is Cardinal Newman's treatise *The Idea of a University*, which was first given as lectures at the University of Dublin in 1852. Newman had been a Protestant, became a Catholic, gave many sermons, taught and was rector at a university, and wrote many tracts that intervened in public religious issues. His defence of the university was religious but not denominational. Moreover, it claimed to incorporate the classical, pre-Christian tradition within itself. Newman defended what we would today call the "liberal arts," "liberal studies," or "the humanities," in the following terms. "This process of training, by which the intellect, instead of being formed or sacrificed to some particular or accidental purpose, some specific trade or profession, or study or science, is disciplined for its own sake, for the perception of its own proper object, and for its own highest culture, is called Liberal education." It is not that there is anything wrong with training for a definite job. It is simply that we all, as humans, have a higher calling: to use our minds to strive towards the highest cultivation of which we are capable. Newman allowed that all branches of knowledge and science were a valid part of the university, but he considered them, precisely, as *branches* of a unified knowledge imparted by both philosophy and religion, and leading to the "true culture" of liberal knowledge. In this sense, the liberal arts are the core of the university. It should be clear to us that this was always an elite, aristocratic ideal. Not only workers and peasants, but the shop-keeping middle class also, were too preoccupied with immediate survival to spend years in self-cultivation.

Over time, Newman's ideal has been very much sec-
ularized, as has society in general. An important step in
the process of secularization was when Matthew Arnold
took the ideal of liberal education away from its ground-
ing in Christianity and based it directly on culture. This
was largely a matter of emphasis: Newman used the term
culture and Arnold noted the importance of the concept
of perfection for culture in Christianity. In *Culture and
Anarchy* (1869) Arnold defined culture as the pursuit of
perfection that is apparent in both beauty and intelligence. Education through culture gave order to character
and thereby to society at large. In Canada, the shift from
Christian religion to culture as the basis of liberal studies
occurred about the same time not only in theology but
also in classics and English and, in large part, accounts
for the centrality of English language and literature in
Canadian universities. Arnold's writing became a key reference point for this shift. The important thing here is
that the basic conception of the value of a liberal education survived the shift in emphasis from its basis in
religion to one in culture and would later successfully
survive a transition that set aside religion entirely for a
secular foundation.

One element that is at the forefront of Arnold's
conception that is absent in Newman is that culture is
defined from the outset in opposition to civilization.

Our civilization is, according to Arnold, "mechanical and external" and "faith in machinery is our besetting danger." In this context a liberal education takes on a more political role, if we understand "political" to refer to addressing the basic conflict of one's time. Arnold understood this through the opposition between inside and outside. Spirit and culture were taken to be internal and mechanical organization external. Thus culture, in developing the character internally, was the basis for criticizing the merely external and mechanical organization of society. "Culture begets a dissatisfaction which is of the highest possible value in stemming the common tide of men's thoughts in a wealthy and industrial community, and which saves the future, as one may hope, from being vulgarised, even if it cannot save the present." In Newman's time, and generally before nineteenth century industrial capitalism, liberal education was understood in opposition to ignorance. For that reason it was essential to one's character from which one's participation in society grew. All of this was "the good life" as the Greeks knew it. With the addition of Christian piety this ideal formed the tradition of Western humanism that is preserved in the liberal arts. By Arnold's time, industrial capitalism had rendered social organization mechanical and artificial (in the language of the time). Liberal education thus took on the additional burden of not only opposing ignorance but also opposing this form of social organization that was accepted as normal by the ignorant. Whereas previously the learned and the ignorant existed side by side and could be expected to continue to do so, in the nineteenth century "ignorance" had become a powerful social force threatening the educated. Those schooled in the liberal arts had therefore to protect themselves, and the ideal of liberal education, by criticizing external and mechanical civilization. The dissatisfaction with ordinary life, which education must always instil, was no longer simply oriented to the individual's escape into a cultured elite, but toward changing — or at least holding at bay — the organized force of ignorance.

THE CONTEMPORARY UNIVERSITY

There is, then, no single essence of the university; there are three traditions that comprise it: the modern research university based on scientific reason; liberal studies; and professional studies (which I have not mentioned until now). These traditions have been developed differently in different countries. The research university was originally a German invention. Elite Écoles were characteristic of French higher education. Liberal studies were the core of the English university. Professional schools varied according to the demands in various countries. However, these national aspects have become very mixed in recent years. It has been argued that the Canadian model is that of a "public, autonomous, secular, degree-granting institution."

The professional schools—law, medicine and theology—represent a challenge to the most basic feature of the university and can be discussed in that context. Professional schools engage in training to practice a profession recognized within the existing administrative and technical organization of society. They did not claim, at least originally, to advance knowledge. This is no longer entirely the case today, due to the influence of the model of the research university, and it is certainly questionable whether medical research remains dependent on medical practice or whether there has been a reversal in this respect. Theology has, of course, declined with the decline in organized religion through the secularization of society that has led to a decrease in the requirement for priests. Law, though much expanded in contemporary society, remains largely as it began in which theoretical investigations of law are subject to the demands of legal practice. Professional schools have been included in universities for a long time and raise the question of whether universities should do anything more than provide higher training for pragmatic reasons as these schools themselves do. Immanuel Kant had to fight to maintain the ability of the philosophical faculty to write on matters of religion after encountering censorship of his book *Religion*

within the Limits of Mere Reason (1792–93). He accepted
the legitimacy of the faculties of law, medicine and theology but argued that "the philosophy faculty must be free
to examine in public and to evaluate with cold reason the
source and content of this alleged basis of doctrine, unin-
timidated by the sacredness of the object." Free inquiry
always runs the danger of encountering such problems
with what is accounted to be "knowledge" by established
institutions. It needs the ability to ask, in daylight and
not at night, whether such supposed knowledge is really
knowledge at all. For a university to be an institution of
free inquiry, it must place those who ask such basic questions above those who claim to already know the answers
due to their institutional positions. But times change, at
least to some extent. The business faculty plays the role of
the theology faculty in the contemporary university.

We should thus not be surprised when free inquiry
encounters the oppositions of established powers, though
we should defend whatever institutions there are that can
come to the aid of free inquiry. Kant's defence of the university claimed that the essence of the university was the
philosophical faculty precisely because it was not tied to
an institutional location with social power like the professional faculties. But there is a more important internal
reason why the modern university has been susceptible to
tendencies that undermine its humanistic traditions. The

tradition of the modern research and teaching university exemplified by the University of Berlin was directly based on the development of specialized science. The tradition of liberal education reaches back much further and claims continuity with the classical and Christian (also Jewish and Muslim in some places) heritage. It is important to note that the liberal arts were not hostile to science. Initially, and correctly in historical terms, the sciences were seen as part of the liberal arts. Mathematics, physics and astronomy, as well as newer scientific endeavours such as those investigating the circulation of the blood, were undertaken by scientists who were also philosophers, that is to say, scientists who saw their specific researches as part of the traditional search for the good life for humans and perhaps also the glory of God. Both Newman and Arnold saw the scientific passion for knowledge as an essential part of the liberal arts, but the emerging new science with its intrinsic connection to technology gradually burst the limits that connected it to the liberal arts. This central fact has had the long-term effect of separating the sciences from the liberal arts — except the history of science, which is *only* studied within liberal arts and is not of concern to scientists. In fact, it is a condition for the progress of the specialized sciences that they cut themselves off from their past and present themselves to the new generation of students solely through the current state of scientific knowledge. This tendency began in the late nineteenth century. We have already touched on it with the observation that in Arnold's hands the defence of liberal education became a critique of industrial civilization. But Arnold failed to see the extent to which the specialized science of his own day was implicated in the industrial civilization that he opposed. The necessary connection between modern specialized science and technical applications means that science can no longer be held apart from industrial processes. This is even more the case in our own day than it was in Arnold's. It has been captured by the term, and concept, of *techno-science* that attempts to capture the institutional force of scientific research that is intrinsically connected to technical application (see the note on techno-science after the main text). Liberal education cannot help but become a single stream within the modern research university, whereas, according to its own intentions, it would claim to be the *unity* of knowledge.

If the liberal arts tradition has changed its function due to the technological innovations imbedded in the modern research university, it is no less the case that the research university has, for the same reason, abandoned its own ideal of unity. The first university in the United States founded on the German model was Johns Hopkins University (1876). Its inaugural address was given by the eminent English natural scientist T.H. Huxley. He was very much in favour of the research university and its focus on specialization that he associated with free inquiry. In another lecture that he delivered as Rector of the University of Aberdeen, Huxley pointed out that the Scottish universities were more committed to science and practical knowledge than English ones. But, more important than his preference for the German university system, which is perhaps an automatic preference for a natural scientist, is his linking of the practicality of the research university to the aspirations of workers for a better life. One of his most pungent turns of phrase puts it this way: "It will be said that I am forgetting the beauty, and the human interest, which appertains to classical studies. To this I reply that it is only a very strong man who can appreciate the charms of a landscape as he is toiling up a steep hill, on a bad road. What with short-windedness, stones, ruts, and a bad pervading sense of the wisdom of rest and be thankful, most of us have little enough sense of the beautiful under these circumstances." Well said, surely. It sets up what I regard as one of the most important and problematic alliances of our time: the defence of specialized science with the desire of the working class for a better life. This amounts to an argument that workers should accept the scientific research ideal because it will lead toward better jobs and increased leisure.

It seems that, on the whole, workers have indeed accepted this argument. To the extent that they have, they have bought into one of the major forces that is now undermining the university. The confinement of workers' education to job training, however, was something that was fought by the workers' education movement on the grounds that they have the right to assume the heritage of society and not remain simply the instruments of the powerful. In other moments, such as when talking to such workers, Huxley recognized this point. While people need jobs, and therefore training for jobs, if this necessity is allowed to overwhelm the university, then the higher self-fulfilment and self-knowledge that education promised will be kept forever beyond the reach of the working classes. Leisure, yes, but what is the purpose of leisure, just inactivity, or perhaps shopping? Aristotle had argued in ancient Greece that philosophy requires leisure and is thus confined to the aristocratic class. Modern society, by way of contrast, holds out the possibility that working people may come to enjoy leisure also. But this noble goal has been plagued by a cruel irony: leisure has come in greater degree to workers at the same time that the purpose of leisure — self-knowledge, self-fulfilment, self-expression — has been denied to them in education. The task is surely to combine practical learning with a higher mission.

To be self-knowledge, knowledge must first be a unity. To be a coherent institution, and not just a jumble of remnants of traditions and ad-hoc improvisations, the university must be a unity. That it why it is, or was, called a *uni*versity. These issues came to a head in the 1960s, when several presidents of major universities suggested that it should now be called the *multi*versity. The point of this term is to underline the fact that the contemporary university has no centre and no unity. It is simply the sum of a number of parts in which each part dances to its own tune. A fine face was often put on this change. For example, it was claimed that "as in a city, there are many endeavours under the rule of law." But there was a less benign side to it. The President of the University of California noted that "intellect has also become an instrument of national purpose, a component part of the military-industrial complex." "A multiversity is a translation into academic terms of an affluent society's passion for power," the President of the University of Toronto admitted. The size and complexity of the university was noticeable by everyone, leading to issues of alienation and machine processing of students, but the issue was more basically one of what purpose the university was to serve. Both these presidents, and I am sure many more, spoke then, as they speak now, of simply adapting to the society they serve. It is in this very succumbing to the demands of society as it is, with its great organized pursuit of power, that the recent abandonment of the humanistic ideal within the university itself began — at first by university administrators, but later gathering momentum by adding all the "realistic" voices that suggest that the university should simply serve society in its existing form. Such adaptation to the existing situation, rather than evaluating it and perhaps resisting it and proposing alternatives, is exactly what abandoning the humanistic ideal amounts to.

The student movement of the 1960s rejected the defence of the multiversity and renamed it the *knowledge factory*. In opposition, it argued for, and attempted to create, the democratic university. This argument tended wrongly to assume that the democratization of society and the democratization of the university were simply parallel and indivisible processes, thereby occluding the real differences between them. This mistake was rooted in the Marxist class analysis — which predominated in the student movement of the time — that suggested that there was really only one central power struggle in society. The implication was that the university could only serve either the owners or the workers. Nevertheless, the 1960s student movement made a significant contribution both to the critique of the university's actual functioning in the corporate capitalist world and to the possibility of redirecting it toward enlightenment both within the university and in its larger social function. This ideal of the *democratic university* continues to motivate the critique and proposals that I make in this book even though its meaning (I will argue) has to be more through a renewal of the university's function of public reflection than in a simple choice of sides.

With these historical illustrations, I have been trying to show that the humanistic ideal of the university that was originally held up by both liberal arts and the research university was based on the unity of self-knowledge. Further, I have argued that this ideal has been undermined by the specialized and technically applied dimension of modern science released by the research university tradition. This has pushed science out of liberal studies, except in a historical sense, and has pushed self-knowledge out of the research university. We are left with the remnants of these traditions, not the traditions entire. This is another reason why a conservative critique of the current state of the university will not work. Techno-science, the unification of technical innovation with specialized science, has undermined the major aspect of the university as such: the unity of knowledge. Our task now is to attempt to understand how this explosive element of techno-science is restructuring the contemporary university. I will break this up into three issues: the corporatization of the university, the commodification of knowledge, and the emergence of a new model of knowledge. Most immediately, the university is endangered by the corporate agenda that would reduce it to being simply another public-private partnership and the knowledge it produces to a commodity on the market. But it is also changing in relation to the new nexus of knowledge that is coming into being, a techno-scientific model in which an emerging science-technology-communication unity is undermining the traditional basis of the university. The next three chapters take up each of these issues in turn.

A HISTORICAL OUTLINE OF THE IDEA OF THE UNIVERSITY

The preceding account of the history of the university has attempted to illustrate the way in which the idea, or ideal, of the university has shifted through time and combined into the composite form that now predominates. It has also emphasized how the alliance between specialized scientific research and marketable innovations has undermined the claim for a unity based in self-knowledge. It is hoped that this account provides us with enough of a measure, an ethical standard, that is internal to the university for us to proceed with the evaluation undertaken in the next three chapters. To recall this history, and to summarize it quickly, we can distinguish seven different forms of the university.

The *classical humanistic tradition* in Greek, Latin and (predominantly) Christian forms (but related to Jewish and Islamic knowledge from the same tradition) present in the medieval university, but also in independent scholars and scientists, based on the idea that knowledge—self-knowledge and knowledge of *cosmos* (Greek) or *creation* (Christian)—was essential to living the good life.

The *modern research and teaching university*, after the founding of the University of Berlin in 1810, funded by the state and with a public function. The classical humanistic tradition becomes a current within the humanities and remains somewhat distinct from the modern research and teaching emphasis. The professional schools are incorporated into the university. This operated at first as an *elite university*, in which higher education was for the self-development of the upper class and training for elite jobs in the national bureaucracy or Empire.

The *public university*, a nineteenth and twentieth century invention supported by public funding in a representative democratic polity, that continues the tradition of the modern research and teaching university but grows much larger to accommodate the increased function of knowledge in society, and finally becomes the multiversity. Its public function was an uneasy combination of job training and citizenship.

The *multiversity*, an unstable and transitional state between the public university and the corporate university that adapted to the explosion of knowledge-based innovations relevant to corporate profit-making and at-tempted unsuccessfully to maintain the public and classical traditions of the university in balance with techno-science.

The *democratic university*, a never-realized ideal proposed by the 1960s student movement as a critique of the multiversity and also held by many who work in the university and see it as an agent of enlightenment not only through teaching but in its wider social role.

The *corporate university* that, due to fiscal cutbacks and the ideology of privatization, undermined the public university beginning in the 1980s, including the surviving humanistic tradition, and by the new millennium had become the new university structure.

The *network university*, an emerging new form of, and role for, the university in the network society, which is based on techno-science. (To be taken up later.)

It should be recalled, however, that reality is always more muddled than the clarity that can be expected from concepts. These concepts that can be derived from a historical account are needed to provide the evaluative context required to measure the reality of the contemporary university. The actual university, however, still contains survivals of earlier forms as well as anticipations of new developments.

CHAPTER IV

THE CORPORATE UNIVERSITY

The major humanistic traditions of the university that interpreted self-knowledge as either the knowledge an individual needs to live well or as citizenship (or as both, of course) did not have much connection to economic activity or well-being. Thus the humanistic and economistic ways of life could, and did, exist alongside each other in modern society for a long time, characterized, from time to time, by either mutual indifference or hostility. To some extent this was also the case within the university, where the science faculties adapted much earlier to the corporate world and the arts faculty continued to draw on older traditions. There have been attacks on the humanistic university before, but now it seems that they have finally become successful. I can see two reasons for this. First, funding from the nation-state has been seriously cut back to the extent that survival, at least in its current form, demands that the university look elsewhere for support. Second, two tendencies from within the university have made common cause with the corporate agenda. The professional faculties have always had a primarily pragmatic orientation and, in a corporate climate, turn toward a corporate understanding of utility. Also, as I have outlined, technical application of specialized knowledge is a source within the university of the pull toward the corporate world. Moreover, the corporate world, though it has its own research and development centres, sees great advantage in annexing the university to its own interest in profit making. Every society projects an image of itself that it finds largely self-evidently legitimate and convincing. It should not be found surprising that in a corporate culture it is self-evident to many people that universities should be run like corporations. What is at stake in this?

THE GLOBAL CONTEXT

Our historical survey showed that the modern university has been primarily publicly funded. The king, the republican or parliamentary system, contemporary mass democracy — whatever the system of rule, the institution that stood for the public political power instituted and maintained the universities. To be sure, private universities have existed (in the United States more than in other countries). However, even private universities in this context were expected to play a public function in addition to their private one and most of them received tax relief from the state even if they didn't receive direct subsidy. They were not intended to be profit-making institutions even if they were private. On the other hand, the new for-profit private universities, pioneered in the United States in the 1990s but now spreading beyond it, are designed to produce a profit for their shareholders — much like any other joint-stock company.

If we picture society as a map of institutions connected by relations of power and influence, it would look something like this: the capitalist economy and the nation-state are the most powerful institutions in modern society. They provide the funding base for most other institutions and/or exert an influence on all other institutions due to their ability to set "the rules of the game." The university was generally publicly funded and therefore to a large extent under the influence of the nation-state. The university operated in a capitalist economic environment. Capitalist enterprises paid a lot of the tax revenues available to the nation-state to fund universities. They were the main place in which workers and professionals trained in the universities could find work. This is not to say that the university was simply a plaything of the state and the economy. It had its own priorities and structures. However, the university's own inner structure had to be articulated within this wider environment in a sufficiently successful manner to ensure its survival. One major reason for its success in this regard was that both the state and capitalist enterprises were aware of the increasingly important role knowledge-based technical applications played in industry. This was in addition to the traditional role that the university played in training administrators for the state. Training of workers and professionals was clearly an important prerequisite for remaining competitive on an international level. There were other reasons as well. Scientific research added not only to the practical advantage of industry but also to the prestige of the nation-state. Such prestige was also enhanced by the national literatures taught at the university that were added to the classical liberal arts as a sign that the modern nation-state carried on the great Western classical tradition.

The modern university survived and prospered at the intersection of the dominant institutions of the nation-state and capitalist economy because it knit together, legitimated and aided them. The basic condition for this situation was what we may call the *national economy*. Capitalist enterprises operated primarily within a specific nation-state and, even when they operated abroad, the headquarters of the enterprise was national. Capitalist enterprises were therefore dependent on the prosperity of the national state and their influence upon it. There was, during the period of the national economy, a certain harmony between these two dominant institutions that supported the role of the university as a quasi-independent institution.

There has been much debate on the historical periodization of the national economy. Also, some analysts have pointed out that the national economy was never entirely national, and others, that the globalized economy still has some national roots. However, what is important is that, as is common knowledge now, the capitalist economy is now not only of global reach but its major capitalist institutions are neither tied to, nor dependent on, the nation-state. Global capitalist corporations exert an influence on the nation-state, not because they are regulated and taxed by the nation-state, but because they control the global environment within which nation-states must survive. From the standpoint of the contemporary global economy it is possible to look back and define a previous state of affairs called a national economy in which the nation-state was the context for the capitalist economy, rather than the reverse. It is important to understand that the modern university was designed in this situation. The public funding that contributed both to advanced training and national prestige also served the capitalist economy. The public function of the traditional modern university is based on its role at the intersection of state and capital in the national economy.

With this background in mind, it is relatively easy to see why the university has had so much difficulty in recent years. Capitalist corporations have shed their dependence on the nation-state and now exert a pressure from outside for the state to conform to the global capitalist economy. Corporate taxes have fallen everywhere and the financial basis of the nation-state that supported the public function of the university has been withdrawn. At the same time, the rationale that university education produces better-informed citizens has been in decline. The humanistic ideal has fallen on hard times: if self-development is just for yourself, why shouldn't you pay for it? For at least twenty-five years, the university has been refashioning itself to fit into this new environment.

What are the signs of this fundamental change? One sign is that universities have scrambled to give themselves a brand name so that they, and their products, have a distinctive visibility in the education market. The web sites, stationery and signs all bear the brand name: "Thinking of the World" (Simon Fraser University), "Redefine the Possible" (York University), "Canada's Answers to the World's Questions" (University of Toronto). Though perhaps this exercise is only for those universities whose name is not already a sufficiently well-known brand: Harvard University and the London School of Economics and Political Science don't have a slogan on their web sites.

Another sign is the emphasis on intellectual property. Like similar developments at universities around the world, Simon Fraser University professors' bi-annual reports on their activities now include several pages devoted to what innovations are being worked upon and the intellectual property measures and agreements that cover them. This is largely a source of humour to humanities professors like myself who have nothing to write in these pages. But it is not a joke that this has become so important that it is included as a standard section of considerable length, now dwarfing those sections devoted to publications, teaching and other traditional academic activities. It is clear that it is no longer publicly available knowledge that is important but privately owned and controlled innovations.

If the university no longer resides at the intersection of nation-state and capitalist economy, where is it located? The university's previous location in the national economy meant that it was dependent upon and served two masters. Sometimes there was surface tension between the capitalist economy and the nation-state but there was a more basic harmony of function. The university produced both higher training and a national rationale for these masters.

These functions were integrated with and based upon the three internal university traditions: the research university, the liberal arts and the professional schools. In other words, the university's function as a *dependent* institution harmonized with its *internal rationales* such that it could play a quasi-independent public role. It served through its independence. What has changed is that this public role is no longer supported by the capitalist economy once it has become global. The cost of higher training can be passed back to the worker or professional because corporations can draw their workforce from anywhere. Reduction of tax income puts the nation-state in a difficult position in financing public enterprises such as universities. Greater movement of people has undermined national universities' prestige; one can hire workers and professionals with degrees from the best universities in the world. In short, the university no longer plays its previous strategic function of legitimation of the *national* economy.

The university is cut loose from its dependence and its legitimating function simultaneously. It becomes another public-private partnership on the economic scene. The university is run like a corporation because it has become a corporation. It works within an economic world for its own purposes. It finances its process of production and offers its product on the market. It does not *serve* but *operates.* This is why many recent critics have been able to point to the emptiness of the contemporary university's slogans and rationales. Bill Readings pointed to the remarkable vacuity of the rhetoric of "excellence" that is pervasive nowadays: excellence at nothing in particular and anything whatever. It is part of the constant search for niche markets, nothing more. Prestige generates what is called unashamedly "cultural capital" that universities use to their advantage in competing with others in the education market. Anything else, it is said, condemns them to failure, irrelevance, or, worst of all in a competitive market, shrinking in size.

THE CORPORATE MODEL OF EDUCATION

If the university has come to function like a corporation, perhaps we should first ask how a corporation functions. A corporation is a private organization owned by its shareholders, for whom the corporation's activity is expected to produce a profit. The responsibility of a corporation is to its owners exclusively. Any responsibilities imposed by the state by law or to the public due to a necessity to maintain good public relations are strictly instrumental to its main goal of producing a profit. The managers of the corporation organize its process of production and the workers carry it out. Whatever the corporation produces becomes a commodity for sale on the market to consumers who, in this age of advertising, must be persuaded that they want this product and that it is superior, or at least a better buy, than other available alternatives.

These four main groups seem a bit fuzzier when applied to a university. Only the managers and the product are easy to spot. The university administration has come to function like management. The product might seem to be education, or learning itself, but this can't actually become a consumer good. The consumer good is the degree, the credentials that the university can issue and which is a scarce good in the sense that not just anybody can decide to function like a university. One needs a licence from the state. (It is interesting to notice that the accreditation of universities by the state has become both more general and more lenient over the last decades.) But: Who are the owners? Are the workers the faculty, the support staff, or the students? While the support staff is essential to the university as a large institution, their activity is to support the main activity of the institution not to undertake it as such — much in the way that an automobile factory needs a payroll department and a cafeteria. They provide necessary support to the main activity of the organization but they do not do it themselves. There are fuzzy cases, of course. Those who order the auto parts that are to be assembled are necessary to the immediate process of production, much as the support staff who keep track of students' courses and grades are necessary to producing the credential. But if the main activity is producing credentials, then the workers are in the first case those who are immediately involved in producing credentials: faculty and students. Faculty are supposed to "impart information" and students accept it. Together they "process the information" that is made available to transform it into usable knowledge by the students. The difference between them is, of course, that students pay tuition ãnd are graded while in search of a credential, whereas faculty are paid and do the grading of students. Faculty collectively decide who receives the credential and who does not. The faculty are workers in the process of producing graduates with credentials. Also, the credential is attached to a specific student; it cannot be bought and sold by itself. So, we may say that to some extent the student him or herself is the product: the raw student is transformed to be a credentialized graduate. The student is both a worker and the product. Who are the owners, the shareholders? Since students take their credentials and sell them on the market, it has to be said that students are, to some extent at least, the owners of the product and thus shareholders in the corporation. The price of their stocks is paid as tuition. The government also puts money into the knowledge factory, so they are also owners. In a democratic political system such as ours, one way in which the government maintains its legitimacy with

the voting population is by supporting higher education whereby the population gains access to better jobs
in the knowledge-based economy and, one expects, better
wages. So, I would define the five groups of the university
on the corporate model this way:

Owners = taxpayers (through government) and students
(and/or parents)

Managers = university administration, connected to the
Ministry of Education

Workers = faculty and students

Product = students with credentials

Support staff = all those necessary functions not immediately
connected to producing students with credentials

Since the university is a public-private enterprise,
and not simply a private one, it does not produce a profit,
as such, for its owners. It produces a socially recognized
good, a use value, for which the owners are willing to
pay themselves. The concept of a "use value" used here
refers to something which is useful to someone but which
doesn't necessarily have a price attached to it. Oil, for
example, has a price (or exchange value) and is also useful for making into gasoline or for other purposes (which
also have prices). But health, for example, is useful even
though it doesn't have a price. Activities, such as making dinner, can be useful without having a price—even

though the same activity carried out in a restaurant does have a price in the wage paid to the cook. A hospital has a price in what it costs to build and maintain, but its product is health, which is a use value only. Healthy people can't be bought and sold on the market, but health is a use value that is socially recognized (in a certain way and to a certain degree) and is paid for by those who fund the health system (taxpayers and clients who pay for extra services). It could even be said that health is a use value that enables workers to sell their labour for a price, even though it isn't the health itself that is sold. Similarly, credentials are recognized use values that aid the students in selling their labour on the market.

So, when we hear today that "education has become a commodity" we should be a little cautious and ask about its exact meaning. If it means that education has become completely permeated by the market system, then it is true. But a commodity is defined as something that can be bought or sold on the market (and therefore has a price) and education can't be simply bought and sold. Even these new phony universities that sell degrees, often based on the flimsy excuse that they count "life experience," sell credentials with students' names on them. While the so-called university makes a profit by selling credentials, the credentials themselves aren't commodities but use values that increase the market value of graduates' labour. If the graduates can't get a job then the credential does nothing for them. The credentials are not themselves use values but characteristics of the graduate that affect their potential on the market. They are something like intelligence, personal attitude, clean fingernails—that is to say, personal characteristics that affect their market outcomes, not market goods themselves. This is because, even on the market model, the credential cannot be separated from the person who has the credential. In that sense, a credential itself is not a commodity. (We will see in the next chapter that the situation is rather different with technical innovations produced by university research since they do have a market value.)

EDUCATION AS A CONSUMER GOOD

How does university education work when it has become a public-private enterprise? It does not produce a good that serves a more powerful institution outside itself; it functions itself to produce a good that is socially recognized as a use value such that its owners, or future owners, are willing to pay for it. Basically, the university succumbs to the consumer model of education. Since it produces credentials that graduates use to improve their labour's market position, it must sell itself to those people as a useful good. Our corporate society delivers useful goods to consumers through the market. I will describe the

functioning of education as a consumer good with emphasis on the three main groups that constitute the university:
administration, faculty and students. (I leave support staff
out of consideration here not because they are not important to the running of the university, which they are, but
because their functioning hasn't really changed under the
new regime, even though the intensity of their work has
certainly been increased with fiscal cutbacks.)

University administration has changed drastically in
the last couple of decades in its wholesale acceptance of a
corporate management model. Since higher representa-
tives in the university — Chairs, Deans, Vice-Presidents
and President — are usually elected positions, there used
to be a continuous movement in which faculty members
took these higher positions and then returned to their
teaching and research positions. This movement kept
administration close to faculty and management functions, at least ideally, subordinate to the specific mandate of
the university as entrusted to the faculty for safe-keeping.
Nowadays, once a faculty member enters administration
he or she is unlikely to return to teaching. The department Chair position functions as a sort of apprentice-level
training for administration. There is an inter-university
movement among administration at the Dean's level and
above that is facilitated by employment and head-hunting
agencies. Whereas department Chairs used to represent

the faculty to the administration, they increasingly represent the administration to the faculty. That is to say, the university is becoming a top-down, hierarchical institution on the corporate model. Accordingly, administration salaries have become very high, like those of corporate CEOs and management.

Along with this structural change, the business model predominates in decision making. The number of students taught per dollar spent is the basis on which educational programs are begun or cancelled. If students do not want to take a difficult prerequisite course, there is pressure to make it easier or eliminate it. When embarrassing issues of principle are raised, everyone waits politely and then resumes business as usual afterward. Professors themselves often succumb to this logic after finding that arguments based on long years of experience in teaching and research have been pushed aside for the bottom line. It is no wonder that administrators now find no difficulty in selling monopolies on consumer vending of soft drinks on university premises to Coca-Cola or some similar corporation, effectively appropriating the needs of students, faculty and staff as a private source of income.

If administrators have become managers, students have become consumers. Ironically, this has to some extent given students a stronger voice in universities — though only within the mass consumer model. Students as much as faculty have great difficulty in raising issues of social importance and principle within the university. The most singular fact about student life in today's university is the shift in payment for university education from the state, or society at large, toward a greater proportion paid by the individual student. This change is consistent with the notion that the purpose of education is to provide credentials for the individual student. Students now carry an immense amount of individual debt and most of them work part-time or even full-time jobs, usually low-paying ones, while studying. This financial burden and lack of time constitutes another pressure toward choosing studies whose credentials produce a greater chance of well-paying work after graduation. This undermines the opportunity for a student to encounter the search for "knowledge for its own sake" while attending university.

The university as a whole shifts its weight and prestige toward professional faculties such as business, medicine, and law. Other faculties select and often carve out those studies with a comparable market potential, such as criminology, communication/journalism, management and leisure studies—not to mention the growth of studies like food preparation, hotel management, and police studies that, while they involve necessary training, are utterly foreign to, and out of place in, the university. Over time, the traditional core of the university has come to operate in a hostile atmosphere that neither appreciates nor cares about its traditional function. Once its function becomes simply training, any sort of training can claim entry into the university.

For most students, university life has become continuous with work and preparation for work. They often don't have time to do the reading for their courses and sometimes can't even attend class regularly due to work commitments. They just don't have the distance from work life to engage in the reflection that university studies traditionally required. The university has adjusted, though mechanically and without due consideration, so that requirements have become more lax, expectations have lowered, and education has degenerated toward the simple "transmission of knowledge." Teaching methods have been skewed toward entertainment and over-simplification. PowerPoint presentations put the class notes up for all students to read and copy, thus eliminating any necessity to think about what the professor is saying. Dumbing down is the order of the day, so much so that students seem to think that just attending class should be worth a B grade.

These developments have produced enormous pressure on professors. Most of them studied under a previous system and were attracted by the university in its more traditional guise. They feel baffled by students who have no deep interest in what they are teaching and are often given to severe criticism of contemporary students—though many also simply shake their heads in frustration when they consider the outside work and financial burden that students bear. Real education takes time and sufficient distance from daily worries to think things through. At the same time, professors' own conditions of work have been radically transformed.

In the first place, the intensity of work has increased. Computer use has downloaded much work previously done by support staff onto individual faculty. The amount of bureaucracy and reporting procedures has significantly increased. Classes have become much larger. The introduction of "performance indicators" to measure faculty efficiency has skewed the understanding of faculty work toward objectivistic, abstract measures and away from self-evaluation based in the teaching and research experience. Stress-related diseases are on the rise. In short, faculty have moved away from being individual scholars toward being workers within a large bureaucracy. Second, market factors have come to influence the nature of faculty work. So-called market equivalent payments have skewed faculty salaries. Those faculty whose speciality has some equivalent in the market economy are paid higher salaries than other faculty. This mainly affects faculty in such areas as business, management, computer science, engineering, some areas of science, etc. Not only is this an undue strain on university resources, but it skews the university budget toward certain market-related activities and away from others. Within arts and social sciences it is primarily economics and criminology that are eligible for market equivalent payments. For example, in 2009 approximately 60% of faculty at Simon Fraser University were being paid market equivalents, comprising virtually all recently hired faculty outside the Faculty of Arts and Sciences. This practice downgrades the choice of university teaching and research as a vocation undertaken for its own specific characteristics and rewards. The conception of a university professorship as an ethical vocation remains strong only within those areas distant from market application. Third, the ability of a professor to obtain external funding for research has become a factor in tenure/promotion and merit pay decisions, which cedes university autonomy in determining work well done toward funding agencies with their own agendas.

Alongside these changes in the nature of academic work, there has been a significant change in the form in which the work is organized. There are many fewer tenure-track faculty members and an immense increase in part-time, contract and sessional faculty. These people are fully qualified — many have doctorates and years of teaching experience — but are paid only per course or per session for teaching. The pay is very low and there is no consideration for research or publication. This development amounts to the creation of a two-tier workforce in which the lower level lacks almost all of the benefits normally attached to university work. This development can be seen as a strategy by university administrations to lower the level of pay for university teaching without confronting the existing tenured faculty. In time, these older faculty will retire, few will be replaced, and the nature of university teaching will be utterly transformed with hardly a peep. Some estimates suggest that in the United States, where this tendency is more advanced, 70% of those teaching in universities are in this category. The current figure for York University in Toronto, which seems to be leading the trend in Canada, is about 55%.

The creation of an underpaid workforce devoted strictly to teaching reinforces one of the most worrying trends of contemporary corporatization. What distinguished university teaching from that of other levels in the past was that university teachers were also researchers, thinkers and writers. They were involved in knowledge *production* not just transmission. A field of knowledge is seen very differently by a person who is in the process of contributing to its current state than by someone who simply accepts that current state as given. University teaching was a preparation for students to become knowledge producers and it was thus necessary for them to experience through the university researcher/teacher an *active* organization of a field such that currently interesting questions could be advanced by further research. The tendency of the corporate university is to reserve the function of knowledge production for a few elite scholars and confines the vast majority to knowledge-transmission. In the summer of 2009, the presidents of five major Canadian universities launched a campaign to change university research funding such that they alone would pursue "world-class research" and all other Canadian universities would be confined to undergraduate teaching. This proposal is only the tip of an iceberg that we have been approaching for some time, which would change, for both faculty and students, the role of university learning. It is no accident that students have become more passive at the same time as the proletarianization of university teaching.

This new division between knowledge transmission and knowledge production is also manifested in the practice of governments naming other sorts of tertiary education institutions as universities. This is a phenomenon that is occurring in almost all countries and under different sorts of governments. In British Columbia, community colleges, where faculty teach about twenty hours in the classroom per week, have been renamed universities without any additional resources or expectation of research or publication. No one with a teaching load that high, who must also prepare lectures, grade papers, meet students and keep abreast of their field, can possibly have any time for research or publication. By naming such institutions universities, the requirement that university teachers be also researchers, thinkers and writers is effectively eliminated. The net effect is to erase the expectation for active research from the university as a whole.

Corporate separation of teaching and research has consequences for the entire function of the university in society. University professors, as a group, traditionally could write for three different audiences (even though each individual would likely choose a different emphasis than others). They wrote to report their specialized research to other researchers with that speciality. They wrote for students, often to aid in teaching. They wrote for the general public to contribute to public deliberation on social issues. In the corporate university this has been narrowed considerably. While a few write textbooks, the majority write only for researchers in their specialization. This has led to public scepticism about the usefulness of publication, but the problem is not with specialized writing as such. It is with the fact that this is becoming the *only* kind of writing produced due to the model of elite research and the severing of university culture from a notion of social responsibility. Public commitment to higher education and writing by university educators aimed at the general public can only be revitalized together.

The tendency toward thinking of higher education as simply knowledge transmission has many consequences: it degrades the education that students receive; it creates a class of university teachers who do not have the ability to advance in their fields because they cannot undertake research; it creates an elite of university-based researchers often beholden to funding institutions in the questions that they pursue; it reinforces the tendency in society at large to think of education as something that one has, or does not have, rather than as something that one *does* and which changes the person who does it. This is perhaps most fatal. There are many issues about which the public needs not only information but about which the public needs to *think*. It needs the example of university-based thinkers writing about such issues to stimulate its own thinking—to raise the bar of public thought in general. The confinement of many of the most educated members of our society to being simply transmitters of knowledge, rather than producers of sustained thinking on public issues, impoverishes the society as a whole and its ability to respond thoughtfully to the challenges of our time.

CHAPTER V

KNOWLEDGE AS A COMMODITY

In the preceding account of the corporate structure of the university, it was the function of the university as *teaching*, that is to say, as producing graduates with credentials that was at issue. But research is another function of the university. The classic modern university was defined by the inseparability of teaching and research, but the corporate model of the contemporary university has separated them so that they require separate analysis. The research product has indeed become a commodity that has a direct market value, unlike the credentials that are inseparable from the graduate. In becoming a commodity, the product of research has changed from being a public good into a private one. The corporate university produces *proprietary* knowledge.

By funding specific research projects, corporations use university researchers to produce innovations that they can exploit on the market. Even if not directly funded by corporations, university researchers now share patent rights with the university and can themselves seek corporate partners for production and marketing purposes. This amounts to a massive subsidy for private corporations by the public funds that go into supporting universities and paying faculty salaries. The research function of the university has succumbed almost entirely to privately owned innovations, whereas the traditional function of the university would suggest that its public funding mandates research and innovation for public purposes. There are some projects that strive to fulfil this mandate even in a hostile environment, of course. For example, the Public Knowledge Project is developing free software for both scholarly publishing and that directed toward a general public in order to develop open access to Internet communication. This is a good example of the publicly beneficial research that is becoming increasingly rare in the corporate university.

Contemporary society is pervaded by knowledge-based innovations of all kinds. Medical research, new drugs, technical innovations, etc. affect millions of people daily. Government institutions of regulation and testing, such as Health Canada and Environment Canada, have been seriously degraded by under-funding such that they often have to rely on privately funded testing to make their decisions. Without an independent body capable of testing the claims of such knowledge-based innovations, the public is left vulnerable. I take it as obvious that corporations who test their own products, from which they intend to make huge profits, are not genuine sources of independent assessments. University-based researchers, on the other hand, have both the expertise and the independence to make assessments in the public interest. Moreover, they are able to raise questions concerning the larger social context and consequences of such innovations (if not hampered by being confined to delimited technical questions). Thus, even under the corporate agenda one can argue that there is a need for publicly oriented, university-based research because it has a greater purchase on the public trust due to its presumed independence. However, at the same time, this independence is being undermined because it tends to raise questions that might challenge the corporate agenda. A politics of the democratic university in the corporate age will have to address this contradiction and, to do so, will have to take its critique and agenda beyond university faculty to the students whose education is compromised by corporate-dominated research and, even more important, to the public whose welfare is sacrificed to it.

This point is perhaps easy to see in the case of medical and technical innovations, but it is no less pertinent to studies in the social sciences and humanities. Relevant thinking about social structures and practices, their history and their prognosis, is required by a democratic society which relies on informed citizens and social actors capable of sensible decisions. There is an important role for academic freedom in a democratic society and a defence of the democratic university cannot prevail unless it reaches the active citizens with which it has a common interest. Social democratization and the democratic university, while not exactly equivalent, cannot ultimately prosper without each other.

ACADEMIC FREEDOM IN THE CORPORATE UNIVERSITY

The modern university has historically played three distinct roles — elite, public, corporate — and has been perpetually haunted by another possibility — the democratic university. These roles have defined the relation between university and capitalist society. However, university structure and functioning does not simply mirror the social-economic environment with which it must come to some accommodation. Similarly, politics within the university does not straightforwardly mirror politics outside. Their complex articulation sets the framework within which democratic politics can today be carried on within the university.

Academic freedom is one way in which freedom of inquiry in the university is tied to freedom of self-expression in society. A conception of the university based in the educative encounter that holds social relationships up to critical inquiry necessarily finds itself in conflict with entrenched powers. The public university gained a certain autonomy by accepting the legitimacy of the corporate economy outside its gates and confining its criticism to the classroom. This bargain was possible through a conception of "spheres of society" in which different principles prevailed. While the university was dedicated to critical thinking, the economy was dedicated to profit making. One has only to remember the outrage that was visited from all corners when this separation was breached. In the 1960s the student movement expected "the critical university" to play a social function also and thereby drew the wrath of both public powers and university administrators whose distance from economic powers was thus threatened. But it is important to remember that the separation was not first breached by the student movement: it was the role of the university in war research, anti-union activities, job training for the corporate elite and its technical lieutenants such as engineers and personnel department flunkies, corporate funding of technological developments, and the failure of its critical function that provoked the student movement's rejection of the separation of spheres. The critique of the "knowledge factory" was a key element of that movement. Indeed, the "spheres of society" seemed only to apply to a restriction of the critical function of the university and not to its increasingly strong ties with corporate and warfare powers. It was an uneasy conception at best, though it offered more independence than the subsequent corporate university ever could. During the 1960s, in a period of expansion of the universities due to the requirements of a more scientific-technical, bureaucratic capitalism, protections of academic freedom became more widespread and extensive. For a short moment, professors were in demand and could expect greater protection of their role. Those who are senior faculty in universities today had their expectations of tenure, peer review, and academic freedom of inquiry and expression formed during this period. It is hard for us to resist a narrative of decline, but one element of resistance must be to understand the greater university freedoms institutionalized in the 1960s as a specific period of gain rather than the natural state that it has often been assumed to be. We must also keep in mind the predominantly individual nature of academic freedom thus understood, though the gains in democratic self-government within the university were of a more cooperative nature.

Academic procedures are the mediation between the actual functioning of the university and the corporate world. These procedures are the result of a history of the university, which has always accommodated itself to the capitalist environment, but at previous stages gained a certain independence from that environment. The history of academic freedom struggles is one major component of this; another is equity struggles. The present demands of corporatization create a pressure that erodes this hard-won independence. Thus, the administration voids procedures and rules of self-government within the university and, when it cannot do this, violates them altogether. Thus, one current task is to defend the rules and procedures within the university that limit the administration's version of corporate rule and also to extend the democratization of the university in light of the principles that led to academic freedom in the first place. All this is based in the educative encounter of the seminar room that animates those with a vision of the democratic university.

What happens when the corporate university violates academic freedom (as they are likely to do in the process of establishing the corporate agenda on the remains of the public university)? It is not for nothing that recent years have brought us a number of academic freedom cases that go to the heart of the functioning of the corporate university. Well, they don't come down to your office and announce that that is what they are going to do. Since there are still vestigial procedures and rules that make such violations look bad, their actions must be rationalized in another way. Since they are, obviously, responsible administrators doing a necessary job, then the fault cannot be theirs. If fault is not theirs, it must lie elsewhere. Thus ensues a frantic search for others at fault. Finger pointing at "troublemakers who do not play by the rules" is essential to the administrative diktat of corporate rule. This phenomenon has emerged in all the recent cases of violation of academic freedom in Canada—Nancy Olivieri, David Healy, David Noble. All have been transformed miraculously and instantaneously from respected academics worthy of high-ranking jobs and research grants into irresponsible troublemakers and charlatans. The logic of the scapegoat underpins the violations essential to the corporate university's transformation of the purpose of the university. If critical thinking is out, then ritual blaming is in.

Here is the logic: the university has procedures that, theoretically at least, rule out non-academic grounds and old-boy connections and rumours. If the administration wants to make a decision based on such rumours, old-boy connections or non-academic grounds, then it must interfere with the procedures. Then, if anyone points this out, they must defend themselves from wrongdoing. (After all, even if rules were broken, they were only doing what's necessary in the current corporate environment.) If they are not wrong in interfering in this way, then someone else must be culpable: the people who pointed out the violation, the committees that made the overturned decisions, most of all, the person whose academic freedom has been violated. The violated one is transformed in an instant into a powerful source of wrongdoing, thus justifying the "special means" that were necessary to avoid this error. Expel the outside agitator! Then our nice and peaceful university will function smoothly again. This strategy works well given the congenital timidity of the professor type alongside the current corporate forces that make it seem the only realistic option.

Such expulsions do not only occur in the publicized cases. They occur also wherever students and faculty overstep the bounds of a narrow specialty to ask more general and universal questions. Keeping everyone within defined and safe boundaries ensures that difficult questions will not be asked. The corporate university cannot openly address such difficult questions, thus it must make sure that they do not arise. Therefore, it promotes and polices a confinement of inquiry to technical questions within pre-established boundaries that violates not only the procedures, but the function and rationale, of the university as an institution of free inquiry. It is a university in name only, and then only because the right to so name is vested exclusively in the government. The culture of compliance that prevails today allows the corporate university to veil its usurpation of the name. The first task is thus to over-step these boundaries, to raise the larger questions, to make the issues public and thus to fulfil the social task of the university by bringing critical thinking to the public outside the university.

The Canadian Association of University Teachers' (CAUT) policy on academic freedom recognizes the connection between social democratization and the dem-ocratic university. Its first point reads: "Post-secondary educational institutions serve the common good of soci-ety through searching for, and disseminating, knowledge, truth, and understanding and through fostering inde-pendent thinking and expression in academic staff and students. Robust democracies require no less. These ends cannot be achieved without academic freedom." Its logic proceeds from the good of society, to the search for knowledge, to the necessity for free inquiry in the search for knowledge, to the necessity for individual commit-ment and expression in this search. Academic freedom is defined in this way: "Academic freedom includes the right, without restriction by prescribed doctrine, to free-dom of teaching and discussion; freedom in carrying out research and disseminating and publishing the results thereof; freedom in producing and performing creative works; freedom to engage in service to the institution and the community; freedom to express freely one's opinion about the institution, its administration, or the system in which one works; freedom from institutional censorship; freedom to acquire, preserve, and provide access to documentary material in all formats; and freedom to participate in professional and representative academic bodies." To this degree, my argument for academic freedom is nothing more than an independent statement of this logic. It defends the individual freedom of academics and its extension into democratic decision making within the university by saying, "Academic freedom requires that academic staff play a major role in the governance of the institution. Academic freedom means that academic staff must play the predominant role in determining curriculum, assessment standards, and other academic matters." However, the CAUT statement does not extend to the social responsibility of the university institution as such. At no point does the CAUT policy return to its point of departure in the concept of social good. In this respect my argument suggests more. Society as a whole, through its dominant powers, always makes decisions, not only about inquiry, but about the application of knowledge. Health and technical innovations, and also social-political ideas, have social applications. One should investigate them freely, but should one remain silent about their application? Is there no concept of academic freedom that pertains to the question of whether the products of free inquiry are being properly and sensibly applied? Certainly, this kind of evaluation always takes place in some form. Powerful institutions such as corporations, governments and the media engage in it regularly. If academic freedom does not extend to the evaluation of knowledge-based applications, then it completes just half its task. The question of "what is a social good?" must be raised in universities and outside them. This is the connection between the democratization of the university and the democratization of society. Without it, academic freedom in the corporate university is just a wizened, empty shell capable only of justifying the freedom of researchers to accept the large grants proffered by private interests. It is sustained by the logic of the scapegoat. A democratic society demands a more lively conception of academic freedom. Its logic must be one of free inquiry and expression complemented by responsible evaluations of the social good and the actual applications of research.

The corporate university undermines academic freedom and self-government entirely. But the possibility of a democratic university respecting individual academic freedom while enacting an institutional social freedom through democratic decision making haunts both the recent history of the university and its contemporary situation. Recalling this history should establish the importance of defending those gains made at an earlier period, but it should also avoid the narrative of decline. The public university repressed, no less than the corporate university, the democratic possibility that is rooted in the respectful give-and-take of cooperative learning in the seminar. This possibility cannot be kept alive without raising basic questions about the meaning and function of the university in a corporate environment and pressing for the greatest possible cooperative autonomy that will sustain criticism of that environment. Nothing less befits the institution of thought.

A NECESSARY ANXIETY

What are my anxieties? First: Teaching and learning emulate the consumer model, which undermines a great tradition of liberal education. Second: The university is a knowledge-based public institution. To this extent, it must not only develop and transmit knowledge but also subject it to evaluation in relation to social priorities and goals. Present tendencies, however, seem to be driving the university to exercise the first half of this mandate at the expense of the second. Knowledge is becoming a commodity, a private good for sale, and the public interest in evaluation is on the wane. Third: The university is an institution committed to enlightenment. This is the basis for its public evaluative mandate. But the study of the humanities in which the project of enlightenment has been based is on the wane, stigmatized for its supposed impracticality. To the extent that the heritage of enlightenment is shoved out of the university, it will become simply another public-private partnership. If the only institution which was specifically designed to hold society and its institutions up to critical analysis ceases to play this function, we may be all fated to fill slots in the corporate or government machine without being able to ask what it is all for. We may be cut off from our heritage as thinking individuals and as a society that responds to thinking individuals. It is somewhat comforting to know that there will always be some individuals who reject this fate and struggle for self-knowledge and social responsibility. They cannot be expected to achieve much on their own, however, if we systematically degrade all those institutions that aid this struggle for a truly human life. The university is one such institution. That is why my anxieties are shared by many students, professors and even some administrators for whom the university is not only a place of work and study but of love for knowledge, thought, and the search for enlightenment—love of the questions, more than the answers, which will always remain provisional.

The corporatization of the university has not gone on without opposition. Unionization of regular and contract faculty has advanced rapidly in recent years, responding to the new conditions of work. This development may slow and perhaps alter the trend to part-time and teaching-only faculty. Also, there have been a number of faculty struggles to regain democratic control over university administrators. Even more important, some underdeveloped provinces in Canada (New Brunswick and Manitoba) have tied an income-tax rebate to student tuition paid if the student remains within the province to work, effectively connecting the personal cost of higher education to social development priorities. These plans are an initial move that could be developed further. Linking the cost of education to a plan for social development and employment, especially in underdeveloped areas, would allow students from poorer backgrounds to study in the area of their choice and contribute socially afterward. Within an even larger optic, it begins to build a base for a relationship between higher education and social priorities that are shared by a community and not dominated by a corporate agenda. All of these developments are important, but the overall success of such measures in establishing the university in its democratic public function depends upon the extent to which the general public takes an interest in, and is willing to fund, independent universities.

CHAPTER VI

TRANSFORMATION OF KNOWLEDGE

The university used to exist in a complex double relationship to the modern state and the capitalist economy—in one sense dependent on them for resources and support and in another sense independent enough to make the claim to know the whole. The university was clearly inside society as a social institution dependent on other, more powerful institutions. But it was also outside society in the sense that its partial independence provided a standpoint from which the whole of society, history, and nature could be represented as a form of knowledge. Knowledge understood as an organized totality—sub-divided but unified in a structural whole—that refers to and *represents* the world is the specifically modern form of knowledge. Knowledge in this specifically modern form confers structure and meaning on the modern university. I have suggested already that this location and mission of the university has changed, though emphasis has been primarily on the social and economic, that is to say, *corporate* factors that have brought this about. But corporate factors are not the only ones at work here. Institutions are also being transformed by the contemporary interpenetration of technology and science—which is called *techno-science*—that has brought about changes in knowledge production and transmission. These factors are always in practice bound up with social and economic forces, but they are not reducible to them. Under any conceivable social-economic regime, the contemporary transformations of knowledge undermine the traditional structure and rationale for the university and require a new, creative response—that is to say, techno-science is a product of modernity and not just of capitalism. Perhaps these changes were well summed up in the recent statement by a United Nations Educational, Scientific and Cultural Organization (UNESCO) official that "the university has lost its monopoly on the creation of knowledge," a statement that has also graced many recent academic discussions of the topic. But this is a negative statement, a summary of what is no longer the case. Difficult as it is in a time of transition such as our own, real understanding requires some positive, content-filled account of the transformations that are underway. That is the topic of this chapter.

The double, inside/outside relationship of the modern university to society meant that the university was both a social institution and a relatively independent standpoint from which the whole (of society, history and nature) could be represented in the form of knowledge. The end of the double relationship means that the university is in danger of being subsumed within society to become exclusively, one-sidedly, a servant of social interests. We can see emerging a university thoroughly immersed in socio-technical networks identical with those of the society as a whole. This indistinction between university and society implies the end of a standpoint from which one can represent the whole in the form of knowledge and the beginning of the production of forms of knowledge that have a directly social function. Knowledge production becomes an action alongside other actions rather than a representation of the whole field of action.

The classic modern university, in its commitment to teaching and research, was based in the modern concept of knowledge: knowledge divisible into specialized domains and yet unified in the role of enlightenment within the individual. The educated individual thus could participate rationally as a citizen in democratic self-government. The social role of knowledge is not imposed on the university from without but is rooted in its own mission. But the specialization of contemporary research, the multiple and diverse applications to which it gives rise, its centrality to economic gain, can no longer be held within the precarious unity of its classical form. We live in a knowledge *society*, not only with the knowledge-based university, and, while social application is constant and unproblematic, the question becomes whether there is any standpoint from which one can think the whole of society, history and nature. But before I can address this basic issue directly, it is necessary to explain more clearly the nature of the contemporary transformation. Since information, or informatics, is the central factor here, one needs to ask two questions: The first being "what is the *form* of information?" — that is to say, what shape is now given to knowledge and its communication? While the second asks, "what is the knowledge society? — what is the society in which this form of knowledge has come to predominate?

THE FORM OF INFORMATION

All human knowledge must be communicated in some way to be a social acquisition and the form of its communication has both an enabling and constraining effect on what is communicated. Societies that did not have writing, for example, developed techniques of storytelling to remember and pass on the major beliefs and knowledge that had been developed over their history. Choral singing often coordinated the processes of communal work so that the rhythm of the song could be passed on to the individual workers. Writing itself has taken many forms: script, which required copying by hand and encouraged closed associations for guarding the scarce manuscripts; printing by moveable type, which allowed the production of the book and thereby its wide distribution; the typewriter, in which the production of an easily readable, standardized copy could be produced by an individual writer; computer-written text, whose digital form and connection to telephone transmission allows wide dissemination and alteration or quotation/sampling of documents. Then there are other media such as television, film and photography. Visual media allow the encoding of more information in a single image: consider the amount of words it would take to describe a single room versus what can be conveyed by a single photograph of it. Different media convey, with different emphases, different aspects of human experience. Clearly, all of these differences between media of communication, and connections between them, can be made the object of a specialized and detailed study. Communication studies, in this sense of the comparative study of different media of communication and their role in the articulation of human experience socially, has become a recognized academic field of study. This is a rather recent development, even though it has ancient roots, that is motivated by changes in the dominant media of communication during the twentieth century.

The classical modern university was based on several interlocking communication media that were, until recently, relatively stable. Professors worked either individually or in research teams that met on a face-to-face basis. They published their results at academic conferences and in specialized journals and monographs to coordinate their research with the current state of the field as a whole. Students, who were being brought up to the current state of research so that they could contribute to it in the future, were instructed in lectures and communicated directly with professors in seminars. Professors also communicated directly with the general public through public lectures, books and, occasionally, newspaper articles. The professor was thus immersed in three sorts of communication—with peers, with students, and with the public—that were each based in media of communication appropriate to them.

From a communication point of view, the university as an institution was centred in the library. The library was the repository of the development of knowledge up to the present; a professor's ability was measured by the capacity to contribute works to the library; students learned through access to accumulated wisdom to amplify and supplement what they learned directly from the professor.

Thus, while the core of researching and teaching was in face-to-face communication and occurred between individuals, the library was the place where the results of face-to-face interactions were coordinated institutionally with the development and current state of knowledge as a whole. It was thus essential that the library be reasonably complete.

Even this short sketch of the communicational structure of the modern university is sufficient to appreciate how much it has changed in a very short time. When I first went to university in 1967 this was still the basic structure in place. Even the new universities recently built in the expansion of the 1960s followed this model. What has changed? The first, easiest, approximation to an answer is "the Internet." The library only survives today by providing access to many journals and books through Internet access rather than having them physically in the library. This development responds to a real need. Library budgets had been strained to the breaking point by the proliferation of publications and, while this problem has not been solved, turning the library into a "portal" of access keeps many universities from losing access to current research. The portal approach, however, skews research toward current works since they are directly available in this way. Older books and journals are often not available. This consequence may change with time as more works from older media are translated into digital form, archived, and made available through the Internet. Even so, such access is only as sure as the technology of access, transmission and storage that backs it up. Since we are still only at the beginning of this process it is hard to predict exactly where it will go in the future.

There are many other innovations in communication that are connected to this. Distance education organized through the Internet has grown enormously at all universities because of its cheapness and convenience. It has become the dominant form, so that regular lectures have begun to seem more like distance education courses in the way that they present information with PowerPoint packages developed on computers and put on a large screen in front of the students. In short, education has come to be seen as the *transmission* of knowledge. We now see education in terms of the dominant capacity of the new media of communication. But knowledge can be transmitted only if it is completed; thus, teaching is now seen as giving students something in whose formation they have no part. It is no wonder that seminars are on the decline. Students wonder what is the point of discussing texts if the professor already knows what's in them. Why shouldn't the professor just tell them?

What is forgotten is knowledge *production.* How does one come to know? What is thinking? How can thinking be concretized into a specific contribution to a field of knowledge? The unique characteristic of universities was that its professors did not simply transmit knowledge but were engaged in producing it and that learning from someone so engaged was qualitatively different than simply receiving instruction in the existing state of completed knowledge.

The most obvious and yet significant fact in all this is that the number and availability of sources will continue to increase. The library potentially becomes of infinite extension in space and thus ceases to be a centre of the representation of the world as knowledge. With this increase will come an increased difficulty in deciding which sources to use and when one can stop looking and begin to draw conclusions. The digitalized Internet archive suggests an unsurpassable and indefinite huge multiplicity of sources. It will become increasingly difficult to say what one *should* read on a given topic. The notion of core texts is likely to wither and the concept of a liberal education with it. It will become more difficult to speak to each other with fewer common references. More discussions will break off with a vague "I haven't had time to get to that yet…" rather than issue in a considered judgment. The danger is the loss of a common language, a language of reflection that creates a pause in action so that action can become more deliberate and focussed when it does take place.

Rather than enumerate the many changes of a similar sort that are occurring, I want to fix on the phenomenon of *information* itself. The basic change is that knowledge has come to be thought of as information. So, one needs to ask: what is the *form* of information? What is the specific way in which knowledge in the form of information alters and selects from the fund of human experience? I want to say two things that may seem at first to be contradictory: information presents knowledge as completed, as finished rather than underway; and information is always incomplete, can be added to by more information. The key to understanding these two claims is what it means for information to become a bit. In what sense is it closed upon itself to become a piece?

Let me put it this way: In*form*ation forms knowledge into bits, pieces that can be added to other pieces. These bits can then be stored, processed, transmitted and retrieved. The bit of information is thus single, closed upon itself, in the sense that it is comprehensible singly. The statement "In 2001, 76% of Canadians in the twenty to twenty-two-year-old age bracket had some post-secondary education," with which I began this book, is a bit of information. Obviously, I am not equating a bit of information with the internal digital structure of knowledge-processing machines, even though my choice of the term indicates that there is some relationship between the two. Digitization is the breaking down of language, communication, into a series of ones or zeros for storage, processing, transmission and retrieval. A bit of information in this technical sense is composed of a series of such ones and zeros. A bit of knowledge in the sense that I am using it here is a similar breaking down of a larger text or discourse into smaller parts for ease of comprehension and incorporation, but it is not digital. It still contains sense or meaning. It still registers with a human subject. Nonetheless, the breaking down of text to bits of information predominates when information has become the dominant form of communication in a society.

Now, of course, knowledge may always be said to be composed of parts and, in that sense, pieces. But such parts are not necessarily bits of information. They become bits only in the form of information, the meta-medium of communication that is information. The condition for this is that they are at once smaller and larger than traditional texts or discourses. "76% of Canadians…" only makes sense within a larger inquiry into the role of higher education in society. In taking it from this context and quoting it singly, I cut up a text to produce a single quotation and discarded the original text (book). This is the familiar, old-fashioned practice of quotation by which scholars refer back to previous works, modify and use their results alongside new research to produce a contribution to knowledge. In speaking of the form of information I want to suggest that this process of quotation, of breaking into parts and recombining in a new context, is happening in a new way. It becomes a bit of information when it becomes self-standing, independent of the context in which it was produced. In my quotation, I respected the original context, though this may not have been apparent to the reader, by matching the original context with the context of my own writing to confirm that they match sufficiently for no distortion to occur in the quotation. In the form of information it becomes dislodged from this traditional matching of contexts and floats singly so that it is no longer a fact nor a quotation but a *bit*. Notice that this matching of contexts is what is taught when one learns from a knowledge producer and not simply a knowledge transmitter. It is inseparable from the process of inquiry itself. Separated from this context the quotation becomes a bit.

But there is another side to the question. Although the bit of information is single and floats in a self-enclosed manner, it is nevertheless still placed within a larger context. That context is no longer the new context traditionally established by the thinker-writer (me, in the case above) but the infinite library that takes concrete form in the Internet. Its larger context is the infinite totality of other bits of information available. Thus, it can always be added to; in fact, at any point there can always be more added. Therefore, the larger context is always incomplete. The bit of information is knowledge presented as completed in the form of the single closed piece in the context of the infinite multiplicity of other pieces that renders it always incomplete.

There is a reversal here of the relationships of (in)completion as they occur in traditional quotation. In quotation, the single quotation is incomplete in the sense that its complete meaning depends on the whole text — the original text, the new text, and the relation between the two. Incompletion is on the side of the quotation whereas completion is on the side of the whole text. In contrast, a bit of information is complete since it is single and closed upon itself, whereas its proximity to other bits through the infinite addition made possible by the Internet renders it incomplete. The larger structure is now incomplete; the smaller structure is complete. Is it any wonder that knowledge has come to mean bits of information?

CONTESTED KNOWLEDGE IN THE NETWORK SOCIETY

In recent years the idea of a *network* has come into increasingly common use in the social sciences and humanities. It is used both as a description of new social and technical relationships and also as an image, or metaphor, for the structure of society as a whole. The network society is that society in which information has become the dominant mode for the storage, processing, transmission and reception of knowledge. Here we must be careful to understand knowledge not in the modern way as the *representation* of the world but as a *constitutive component* of it. Knowledge, as externalized in technologies based in information, has become a central component of the process of production.

One commentator already suggested in 1995 that "the Third Industrial Revolution emerged immediately after World War II, and is just now beginning to have significant impact on the way society organizes its economic activity. Numerically controlled robots and advanced computers and software are invading the last remaining human sphere—the realm of the mind. Properly programmed, these new 'thinking machines' are increasingly capable of performing conceptual, managerial, and administrative functions and of coordinating the flow of production, from extraction of raw materials to the marketing and distribution of final goods and services." I will not attempt to document the extent to which this has become the case but simply point out that it has two related aspects: first, computational technology has come to pervade traditional production processes and alter them in its image; second, the information-processing component of the economy has become the most dynamic economic sector, due, of course, to its importance to all other sectors. The result of this is that a new process of production has come into being whose central core is based on information processing and computation. The financial regulatory circuits of contemporary capitalism, for example, are thoroughly integrated by and based upon information technology.

The technology of information is not an isolated phenomenon but is the active force shaping social possibilities in its own image. Manuel Castells has therefore concluded that "the information technology paradigm does not evolve toward its closure as a system, but toward its openness as a multi-edged network." He distinguishes five aspects of the network society: the first is that "information is its raw material: *these are technologies to act on information*, not just information to act on technology, as was the case in previous technological revolutions." Beyond that, information is pervasive, based on a networking logic, flexible, and characterized by the convergence of technologies into an integrated system. The network society relegates hierarchy, control and repression to merely local features of the system and operates on a logic of linking and horizontal transfer.

The idea of a society modelled through the pervasiveness of information technology completes itself in the idea of a network—a complex open system of lines of influence and nodes of connection, with many different passages between any given starting and ending points, without a centre or a hierarchical overseer, and without any outside. There are two immediate implications of this idea of a network where the university becomes a node within the network: (1) The university is no longer the only, or even the main, site of knowledge production. Those who produce the information technology are the predominant (new) knowledge producers. (2) Since the network has no centre and is subject to no hierarchy, a basic problem is raised about whether the network can be thought about as a whole. Where is the standpoint for reflexivity?

It is no accident that for many commentators the network, with its transversal flows and absence of hierarchy, represents a utopia of social equality, a utopia that seems today to be within our grasp. For others, the loss of reflexivity and the lack of a standpoint from which to judge the whole is a symptom of decline. It is commonplace these days to style the latter as simply conservative and the former as simply liberal or progressive, but the situation is actually more complex. The question of the future of the university has through our preceding analysis been honed into two issues: What is the role of the university when it becomes one of many producers of knowledge in the form of technical innovation to the network? Is there a standpoint for reflection from which the network can be described and evaluated for what it is? In a nutshell, what remains of the university's commitment to public knowledge and to social reflection when it is reduced to being a node within a network?

It is important to keep in mind that while the network is transversal rather than hierarchical, an open rather than a closed system, that does not mean that it has eliminated social conflict and disagreement. The network is constantly changing due to the continuous introduction of new technologies that require changes in social organization. The manner of this social organization is not predetermined and is often subject to social contestation. In short, every new addition to the network raises more than one possibility of its incorporation; the actual manner of its incorporation advantages one group over another. Network society is thus traversed by social movements that struggle with established powers over the direction of innovations. There are many of these movements. Network society is not based on one basic social struggle or conflict but upon an open-ended series of conflicts that are pointed out and addressed by a plurality of social movements.

In fact, it is even a more basic matter than social movements. Because the network is constantly changing, it destabilizes the identities of those who work and live within it, leading to a search for a viable identity within the current state of the network. This anxiety about identity within the network is what coalesces within social movements and drives them to contest specific innovations. The network is criss-crossed by power relations such that struggles over identity influence the actual form of innovations. Each of these movements poses issues about how to understand the current state of the network. These issues have entered the university and pose interesting philosophical and political questions for thinkers. This independence yet relationship between social movements and university-based researchers and teachers is the most interesting new phenomenon that has kept the university alive as a publicly relevant institution. The notion of the *public* is no longer confined to the political institutions of representative democracy, but has become a space of social reflexivity over the form of innovation and its relation to established and emergent powers. The university exercises its best contemporary role when it brings thoughtful reflection to bear on such public issues.

Rather than describe the phenomena that disturb the equilibrium of the network in detail, I would like to emphasize the logic of such disruption, since it is from these sources that the contemporary university can keep alive its public relevance: Continuous innovation in the network produces an anxiety about identity that leads to a search for identity with both individual and social dimensions. Social movements raise public issues about the current state of the network that can be usefully explored by university-based researchers and influence the public through their teaching, writing and expressions in other media. While the network appears to be a seamless pattern of transversal relations, it is actually a tensional pattern in which each relationship can be opened to public debate. What is going on when this occurs?

Let us return to the bit of information from which the network society is built. The bit of information is closed in upon itself but open to an infinity of potential relationships. Similarly, network society does not offer a stable identity to its participants but enlists them in a constantly changing set of relationships. But simply adding on more relationships does not constitute an identity. An identity is constructed when bits of information are connected into a *meaningful whole*. Such a meaningful whole can only be constructed when one's specific location in the network becomes the locus of a totalization, a vision of the whole. To state it in a formula: a node becomes an identity insofar as it embraces its *place*. Information becomes localized as knowledge, which is ultimately *self-knowledge*; the infinite spatio-temporality of the network becomes the lived time in place of a specific identity. This is the contemporary form of self-reflection that could ground a new concept of enlightenment.

Recall that information treats knowledge as a completed thing rather than an ongoing search. Even though the production process of knowledge disappears in information it still takes place in the network society, though off-stage as it were, in the struggle for identity. The network is parasitic on the production of knowledge that it uses as information. Actually, one needs to distinguish two senses of knowledge here: it is certainly possible to produce new innovations through following out the implications of information already present in the network. However intelligent one might have to be to do this, it is confined to the recombination of existing information. Knowledge production, in the pregnant sense in which I am describing it here, refers to the meaningful whole from which bits of information are derived. In this sense, it is inseparable from the construction of identity. The anxiety about identity produced by the network thus motivates a search for self-knowledge that can produce new knowledge and not simply recombinations of information. It is not by attempting to restore a monopoly of knowledge that the university can find a contemporary public function, but by taking seriously the anxiety about identity and entering into the production of self-knowledge. At this point the contemporary function of the university reaches back to touch its humanistic roots. The search for self-knowledge initiated by Socrates takes on a social function in the network society. Here is the connection between our heritage, our contemporary need, and hope for the future.

CHAPTER XII

WHAT IS POSSIBLE?

I'm not going to pretend that I can come up with a quick fix for the situation that I have sketched or that it's entirely clear what can be done in the near or distant future. A lot depends on whether the public, or publics, comes to recognize the role that a real university culture can play in society and demands the political will and financial resources necessary for it to do so. The future remains unknown. One begins from the problems of the present and the heritage of the past in the hope that real alternatives can be designed that would confront the situation adequately. My approach has been *critical* and thus has tried to avoid both conservative nostalgia and progressivist optimism. I have hoped to show that, even while the contemporary tendency is to reduce the university to a node in the network society, the contested nature of contemporary knowledge can be brought to public scrutiny, and that the crises of identity produced by network society can ground a new concept of enlightenment.

I have tried to portray the corporate university as clearly and realistically as I can. Its current form gives only limited opportunity for hope. But it should be remembered that there are remnants of previous forms and ideas within the university. Often these remnants can be productively reused and reformed in a contemporary context. Even so, the corporate university is the emerging reality, a reality that has already largely replaced what preceded it. At the same time, I have described this reality on the backdrop of what preceded it in order to show that the hopes and ideals that many people invest in the university are not misplaced. The university had a mission. That mission was enlightenment. The corporate university brings with it the imminent danger that the ideal of enlightenment will be abandoned. I rush to add that the university has never been the only site of enlightenment. Art, sometimes politics, literature, friendship, coffee shops: people always struggle to understand, to live on the basis of their understanding, not only to find their place in the world, but to bring the things they live through under the measure of their thinking. I believe that this struggle will never leave the human being because it is an essential element that defines the human being as such. Even so, to see an institution whose job it was to preserve and foster this ideal in ruin and disarray is to see the human struggle for enlightenment dealt a serious blow. How can we recover and reinvent this ideal?

In the short term, one can resist the corporate model and call on the remaining resources of regions and the nation-state to protect the legacy of the public university. But I don't think that we can turn the clock backward. The story of the role of the public university with an ideal of citizenship in the national economy contains the moral that it cannot be reinstated in the same form in a global economy. The story of the changes in the storage and transmission of knowledge contains the moral that the library has passed as the centre of higher learning. How can humanistic studies be saved by being transformed? How can they face these new conditions with confidence in its past and a plan for facing the future?

In order to address the question of corporatization of the university I divided the question into three issues: the corporatization of the university, the commodification of knowledge, and the emergence of a new model of knowledge. In conclusion, it is appropriate to address how these three are related in the phenomenon of techno-science. At present, techno-science is driven by the global corporate capitalist society that has predominantly taken a neo-liberal political form. However, there are signs of a social democratic revival in several parts of the world and the global economic depression/recession of 2008 has led governments back to a Keynesian interventionist economic policy. Despite these changes, technological innovations and their social utilization remain substantially unabated. There is therefore some reason to distinguish, as I have, the issues related to corporatization from those related to techno-science itself. Corporatization is closer to political forces that might alter its direction than techno-science, which is deeply embedded in the modern form of knowledge. Thus, while the three issues that I have distinguished are certainly connected in social reality, they nevertheless pose different problems and one can discern different future possibilities in each case. Social reality is complex in this sense: the relation between several factors does not discount their separate logics and the possibility of uneven development between them. In relation to each of these three issues I have defined a core problem and suggested a possible future line of development. Let us recall these now:

The *corporatization of university structure* as a public-private enterprise regards education as a consumer good that is simply transmitted and not produced by faculty. It tends to separate research from teaching and situate it in elite units oriented to technically exploitable knowledge. A continuing influence of the corporate form on universities that operate within corporate capitalist society is to be expected, however the near-victory of this influence in recent times has been due to the fiscal influence of government cutbacks to education and the rise of dedicated corporate funding. A *revival of the public university committed to citizenship* would require greater government funding and, more fundamentally, recognition that education is not merely the transmission of knowledge. It could be supported by initiatives taking further the New Brunswick and Manitoba model of forgiving tuition (and perhaps other) expenses for students willing to work in areas where social and community development is required. Such a revival would require a broad social recognition of the limitations of the corporate model and the significance of an educative model not only in universities and other educational institutions but also for many other social activities. Many social activities, such as work and leisure, can be seen as learning processes in which producing knowledge and communicating it to others are necessarily bound up together. Such recognition would require a large-scale cultural shift in societies that have been fundamentally restructured by neo-liberal doctrines since the 1980s and would begin to create new publics with a different sort of investment in higher education.

The *commodification of knowledge* occurs because of the intersection of modern techno-science with a capitalist socio-economic form. It cannot be displaced even by a large-scale cultural shift such as imagined above, even though its impact could probably be reduced in that way. However, even in a capitalist environment, there is a potential *public interest in academic freedom and public oversight* of the technical and social innovations that emerge from techno-science.

The *transformation of knowledge produced by techno-science* itself renders the university as a node within an information network. Short of a drastic breakdown, the forces that underlie modern techno-science cannot be expected to abate. However, the network society is not without conflict. Crises of identity are produced due to the continuous destabilization produced by constant technical and social innovation. Social movements are their most visible index. These movements pose issues about how to respond to innovations in the network. Public deliberation is no longer confined to political institutions but has become a *space of social reflexivity over the form of innovation and its relation to established and emergent powers.* Some university-based thinkers and researchers have already begun to exercise a new role by bringing thoughtful reflection to bear on such public issues. The core of my argument is that the social movements that emerge in network society create the possibility of new public issues and that the university can become a site for reflection on these issues. It cannot be the only place since knowledge production is now diffused throughout society, but its importance derives from the heritage of thought that can be brought to bear and its distance from vested interests (should that remain possible). This heritage must be made socially available and thus demands publication in some form as well as active teaching. This would be the role of a new democratic university in enlightenment.

Who would pay for such a university? Since individuals benefit, perhaps they can and should pay part of the cost, but to demand that students pay the whole cost would turn the university back into an elite institution. The answer must be, in a general sense, "the public." For the foreseeable future the nation-state could continue to play its traditional role as the guardian of the public interest, especially since representative democracy demands that the citizens receive some benefit from their taxes. But in the long term, it is already possible to see that this will be a declining element of the mix. What other possibilities are there? We must begin to see the word *public* in a transformed sense. Perhaps different representations of the public, like cities and regions, can bring their common interests to bear by subsidizing or forgiving student loans for those who continue to work and reside in their region or by aiding universities directly as a form of social development and employment. The sense of the university as a node among others suggests that social movements, government agencies, and even business entities (especially if they are locally based or operate with ethical limits to their profit motive) might be brought together in funding. There is some freedom in having a plurality of funders and of funding units and research programs rather than specific projects. But the key here is that the research must be non-proprietary and publicly available. We live in an age of contested knowledge and must find a public interest in clarifying, and contributing to, such controversies. Perhaps in this way we might re-encounter the Socratic essence of the university.

The reduction of the humanistic tradition to one stream within the university cannot be reversed. Consequently, the idea of a unity to knowledge based in the university structure must be renounced. But the emerging possibility that I have defined of reflection with public significance situated at the contested sites of network society would require that each researcher struggle for a unity of knowledge, much as crises of identity in social movements require a struggle for a meaningful whole of experience. The institution would have to allow and promote various forms of "struggling toward unity." This would, it seems to me, be a significant reinvention of the humanistic ideal in network society.

All this being said, I certainly don't have the full answer to how the university can survive as an institution of public reflection. A large part of my purpose has been to write an accessible book on the subject because I believe that this question matters not only to those who work in the university, or in education more widely, but to society as a whole. Remember that the teachers of all our children are educated in university and that the circulation of ideas in a society helps or hinders the ability of each individual to think clearly. The full answer will only come from a widespread reflection and debate about the role of higher education in society. I cannot be sure, but I think that a population to whom individual free thought and democratic participation were important would see that a university devoted to the humanistic ideal is a part of that project. I think that parents who are justly worried about how their children can find work and survive would also want those children to have access to the heritage of thought in order that they might not only survive but live deeply and thoughtfully. I think that young adults crave ideas with which they can measure their society and not just find a place in it. I think that older people want to use part of their leisure to understand their lives. In short, I think that everyone needs, and, if sufficiently exposed, wants, enlightenment. I may be wrong about this, but, if so, I can only crawl into my cave to wonder about it. There are reasons enough for despair, but to teach, to write, to think, is to engage in the struggle for enlightenment.

A NOTE ON ENLIGHTENMENT

The concept of enlightenment, like all philosophical concepts, cannot be defined without first entering into a discussion of what it means. A definition can only come at the end of the discussion. But, of course, that wouldn't help the reader who wants aid in beginning to enter that discussion and following its sometimes difficult paths. As a quick entry point, I mean enlightenment to refer to all of those attempts that humans make to form their lives through a relationship to thought. This, in turn, sends us back to those philosophers who have made such attempts and who have left records of what they meant. Enough content for the discussion of humanistic education as enlightenment in this book can be garnered from a quick look at four philosophers or philosophical movements. But it is important to keep in mind that a concept like enlightenment cannot be regarded as finally defined as if it can be once-and-for-all over with. It must be redefined to meet new tasks and situations. Thus it ultimately raises the question of what is the impulse of philosophy that drives it forward in this way to become the enlightening of its time. I only mention this question and cannot address it here.

Socrates (circa 470–399 B.C.) was the first philosopher who turned Greek philosophical speculation about the universe toward the ethical questions of human life. He was tried and convicted in his old age by the Athenian democracy for corrupting the young and not believing in the gods. Socrates took his inspiration from the Oracle at Delphi, whose motto was "Know thyself," which he expressed as "the unexamined life is not worth living" (*Apology*, 38a). It is important to notice the double negative in this formulation: he does not say that the examined life is worth living, indeed to all appearances he remains agnostic on whether life is worth living. Probably this is not a question that a philosopher could answer definitively one way or another. The philosopher can, however, negate non-meaning—the absence of meaning, despair, or abyss—with an inquiry that grounds *a* meaning if not *the* meaning. Though Socrates claimed not to be a teacher (*Apology*, 33b), he engaged in question-and-answer sessions with various people who claimed to know the meaning of justice, piety, courage, etc. The sense in which he was not a teacher is that he could not pass on what he knew; it had to be rediscovered by each inquirer for him or herself. The answer is not separate from the process of inquiry and the process of inquiry is not a statement but a way of life. It is from this source that we receive the meaning of enlightenment as the search for self-knowledge and of all specialized knowledge as unified in self-knowledge: the way of life of the philosopher.

Since Socrates did not write anything, what we know about him comes to us through other sources. The main one of these is Plato (428–348/47 B.C.). He was present at Socrates' trial (*Apology*, 34a) and was sufficiently impressed to spend the rest of his life on philosophy. Plato's first dialogues, such as *Euthyphro*, *Crito* and *Apology*, probably present a more-or-less accurate picture of the historical Socrates—though even here Plato's artistry was at work; they are not simple reports. Later, Plato's own philosophical positions started to affect his portrayals of Socrates, since Socrates continued to be the main actor in the dialogues and, at least more than any other character, represented the philosopher. This poses a problem for interpreters which has continued from Plato's day to our own: how to distinguish the views of Socrates from those of Plato and where to mark this difference in the development of Plato's work. Socrates was also the subject of a comic play by Aristophanes (between 460 and

450–386 B.C.) called *The Clouds* which features, among other things, Socrates hanging in the air above the stage and at the end going up in smoke (lines 215 and 1505). Clearly, the image of the philosopher as an unworldly figure provoking laughter isn't an invention of our own time, though the portrait by Aristophanes likely contains more insight into the popular views of Athens than into Socrates himself. It is significant that this laughter persists into our own time. It is a perennial defence mechanism against the courage and rigour demanded by self-questioning.

The accounts by Xenophon (circa 426–354 B.C.), *Recollections of Socrates* and *Socrates' Defence Before the Jury*, are likely more literal, indeed perhaps too much so, insofar as they seem to describe how Socrates would appear to someone who understood very little of his philosophical questioning—rather as a contemporary philosopher would appear when described in the weekend newspaper—and saw him as a sort of "good guy" who was misunderstood by the democracy. Even in antiquity, Socrates provoked other, though less important, accounts of his life and philosophy by Diogenes Laertius, Libanius, Maximus of Tyre and Apuleius and this list would expand considerably if it were to be brought up to date. There is no doubt that Socrates was a major figure of his time and that the philosophical idea of self-knowledge was interpreted by his critics as laughable or merely an average virtue already in his own time. He has exerted a powerful influence over history, however, as generations of philosophers have rediscovered the power of his simple message. Self-knowledge turns out to be a much more difficult and dangerous affair than it would appear on the surface. It is one way of life among others.

Immanuel Kant (1724–1804) is the originator of the concept of critique as it is used in modern philosophy to describe the limits of any form of knowledge. Kant himself was concerned with the mathematical physics of his time. He wrote *Critique of Pure Reason* to show the inability of this form of knowledge to answer questions of metaphysics — by which we mean questions about ultimate reality that go beyond any possible experience. As Kant says, "all synthetic propositions of pure reason have this peculiarity, that while in asserting the reality of this or that idea we can never have knowledge sufficient to give certainty to our proposition, our opponent is just as little able to assert the opposite" (*Critique of Pure Reason*, translated by Norman Kemp Smith (Toronto: MacMillan, 1965) p. 617, A776, B804). Reason must then be limited in its application to the realm of possible experience since its application beyond this sphere necessarily produces contradictions. In order to show the limits of a form of knowledge one must understand the functioning of that form of knowledge in detail. Thus, comprehension and critique are closely tied together. One should also point out that this does not mean that questions beyond the limit of a certain form of knowledge cannot be addressed in another way, by another form of knowledge. Mathematical physics was the model of knowledge *tout court* for Kant, whereas in contemporary times we are more aware of many different forms of knowledge. Even so, for Kant the questions that were beyond the reach of "pure reason," or mathematical physics, could be addressed by "practical reason," or ethics. "With the pure practical faculty of reason, the reality of transcendental freedom is confirmed. ... For speculative reason, the concept of freedom was problematic but not impossible; that is to say, speculative reason could think of freedom without contradiction, but it could not assure any objective reality to it" (*Critique of Practical Reason*, translated by Lewis White Beck (Indianapolis: Bobbs-Merrill, Library of Liberal Arts, 1956) Preface, p. 3). In other words, while physical science works with the concept of causality, it can neither affirm nor deny the concept of freedom. Ethical action, in contrast, requires the concept of freedom. If we add to this a third thesis that the practice of physical inquiry depends upon our freedom, even though its internal concepts do not, then it follows that even the science of physics depends upon human freedom. "Even physics, therefore, owes the beneficent revolution in its point of view entirely to the happy thought, that … it must adopt as its guide, in so seeking, that which it has itself put into nature" (*Critique of Pure Reason*, Preface to the Second Edition, Bxiii-xiv, p. 20). Thus, without denying the specific procedures and postulates of natural science, humanistic education can encompass natural science insofar as it is a human enterprise and, thereby, an exercise of human freedom. The many domains of knowledge are thus unified through the practical exercise of human freedom and the ethical thought that pertains to it.

Kant's thinking about enlightenment, for which he is probably better known, is based upon this philosophical understanding. His short essay "What is Enlightenment?" defines enlightenment as "man's release from his self-incurred tutelage." He states that the motto of enlightenment is "*Sapere aude!* Have courage to use your own reason!" or better, "dare to be wise, or discern!" which is from Horace (included in the collection *On History*, translated by Lewis White Beck (Indianapolis: Bobbs-Merrill, Library of Liberal Arts, 1963) p. 3). Enlightenment is the public effect of critique and rests upon the prior courage of the one who dares to think for him or herself.

In the twentieth century Max Horkheimer and Theodor Adorno claimed to have discovered a dialectic within the history of enlightenment. Phrased in Kantian terms, they suggested that the growth in physical forms of knowledge based upon causality have undermined the concept of freedom. This, in turn, undermines the basic conceptual structure of physical knowledge itself. In turning the world into an object for manipulation, humans become capable of nothing else than manipulation, and thereby become subjects of manipulation themselves. They say, "men pay for the increase of their power with alienation from that over which they exercise their power," and "just as the myths already realize enlightenment, so enlightenment with every step becomes more deeply engulfed in mythology. ... It wishes to extricate itself from the process of fate and retribution, while exercising retribution on that process" (*Dialectic of Enlightenment*, translated by John Cumming (New York: Herder and Herder, 1972) pp. 9, and 11–12). This dialectic whereby enlightenment is reversed into myth is not a necessary historical process but stems from the social context within which enlightenment operates. Insofar as the social context is still a context of social domination, attempts at enlightenment run the danger of being turned to serve existing, or new, forms of domination. The aim of self-knowledge thus requires that even previous processes of enlightenment be subject to contemporary critique. The lesson of Horkheimer and Adorno's description of a dialectic of enlightenment is to consider every claim to enlightenment not only in itself but also in relation to the social context in which it operates—to make sure, if possible, that no reversal takes place or, if it does, to renew the process of critique. The purpose of describing a dialectic of enlightenment is thus to open anew the process of enlightenment. Critique, in this sense, always serves freedom.

The current of European philosophy called phenomenology that began with Edmund Husserl (1859–1938) and continued with Martin Heidegger (1889–1976) has made several important contributions to renewing the concept of enlightenment in our own time. Husserl's earlier work was concerned to assemble an architectonic of knowledge based upon certain foundations and established through the critical activity of philosophy, but his later philosophy turned in a more radical direction. As he began to investigate how the fundamental evidences of logic were based on original perceptual judgments of individual objects given in experience, he devised a new form of investigation that he called *retrogression*, or *regressive inquiry* (*Rückgang*), and that operated by *dismantling*, or *unbuilding*. Regression involves going backward from finished or accomplished structures, like those of logic, to the primal or original evidences in which such structures incipiently appear in perception. Such an "elucidation of origin" through "the necessary retrogression to the most original self-evidence of experience" puts theoretical accomplishments into question in a new way (Edmund

Husserl, *Experience and Judgment*, translated by James S. Churchill and Karl Ameriks (Evanston: Northwestern University Press, 1973) pp. 28, 47). Husserl put the accomplishments of modern mathematical physical science to retrogressive questioning in this way. Since Galilean science, as he called it, has come to dominate the modern understanding of knowledge, it has deformed, and ruled out of order, questions which it is now important to put onto the agenda—such as the social purpose of science and technology. His regressive inquiry did not negate the accomplishments of modern science, but put into question its dominance as the paradigm of science, and opened up a more basic and radical form of inquiry. Dismantling traces an institution, like Galilean science, back to its origin and thereby releases the possibility of other forms of knowing, and points to a decision to be made. Husserl summed up its significance in this way: "A historical, backward reflection of the sort under discussion is thus actually the deepest kind of self-reflection aimed at a self-understanding in terms of what we are truly seeking as the historical beings we are. Self-reflection serves in arriving at a decision and here this naturally means carrying on with the task which is most truly ours and which has now been clarified and understood through this historical self-reflection, the task set for us all in the present" (Edmund Husserl, *The Crisis of European Sciences and*

Transcendental Phenomenology, translated by David Carr (Evanston: Northwestern University Press, 1970) p. 72).

There is now a phenomenological tradition that has used and developed Husserl's conception of enlightenment through dismantling. Unbuilding (*Abbau*) is the origin of the term destructuring (*Destruktion*) in Martin Heidegger (Martin Heidegger, *Being and Time*, translated by Joan Stambaugh (Albany: State University of New York Press, 1996) section 6). Some translations use the term *destroying* or *destruction,* which are quite inaccurate. Heidegger used this method primarily to take apart the assumptions established by the history of philosophy in order to open up philosophical questioning that could respond to the present situation. Jacques Derrida used the related term *deconstruction,* which was an extension of the work of Husserl and Heidegger, to refer to his own procedure of critical inquiry. One of his statements of its meaning is: "The movements of deconstruction do not destroy structures from the outside. They are not possible and effective, nor can they take accurate aim, except by inhabiting those structures. Inhabiting them *in a certain way,* because one always inhabits, and all the more when one does not suspect it" (Jacques Derrida, *Of Grammatology,* translated by Gayatri Chakravorty Spivak (Baltimore: Johns Hopkins University Press, 1976) p. 24). This tradition of dismantling is essentially a form of thinking backward, beginning from established accomplishments and going backward toward the origin from which they were elaborated. It does not produce anything to replace the accomplishments from which it starts, but frees the thinking subject from subjection to the traditional power of those accomplishments, thereby opening up the possibilities of new, more radical questioning and self-responsible decision making. It is a new movement of critique appropriate to our contemporary world that is organized by many established institutions that often inhibit one's capacity to think or decide freely. (I have given a more thorough account of phenomenology as critique in Ian Angus, "Phenomenology as Critique of Institutions: Movements, Authentic Sociality and Nothingness" *PhaenEx*, Vol. 1, No. 1, Spring-Summer 2006, which is available at <http://137.207.120.196/ojs/leddy/index.php/phaenex>.)

A lot more could be said, of course, but with these four ideas one has a good start on the concept of enlightenment: knowing oneself, critique, the possibility of a reversal of critique, and thinking backwards toward the origin of institutions. To ask about the relation between the university and enlightenment is to ask how it stands with these practices of enlightenment in the university today, that is to say, what is the situation of thought within the institution?

A NOTE ON TECHNO-SCIENCE

The idea of techno-science is based on the integration of technology and science though the model of cybernetics that goes back to Martin Heidegger's groundbreaking essay "The Question Concerning Technology" that was published in English in *The Question Concerning Technology and other essays*, translated by William Lovitt (New York: Harper and Row, 1977). We may distinguish three aspects of techno-science in this essay. First, technology in Heidegger's usage is not the same as either *technē* in the ancient Greek sense of craft or art that has significantly influenced the philosophical tradition or technique in a more modern sense as a single innovation within a larger technological field. Rather, technology refers to a new configuration of practical activity through technical innovation and a theoretical perspective on the world as a whole, on "what is." Second, this new configuration came into being with European modernity, though it has now become a planetary phenomenon. It is both systematic-theoretical, due to its basis in the new mathematical natural science of the seventeenth century, and committed to continuous technical innovation due to its intrinsic relation to experiment. This dual configuration gives it an unlimited character: nature becomes simply a resource for the activity of techno-science, thereby breaking down the sense of limit or goal (*telos*) that in the Greek view limited human activity within the bonds of nature. The problematic character of planetary techno-science stems from this loss of limit. Third, Heidegger defined technology as a "mode of revealing" and thereby broke down the separation between science and technology in order to see technology not as an application of science but as a force in the production of knowledge. Technology becomes the primary phenomenon through which we see and understand the world and itself is the generative phenomenon behind science.

Heidegger's view of technology, which makes it the last stage of metaphysics in both philosophy and society, has become a constant point of reference for subsequent philosophy. I can here mention only a few developments that are pertinent to the current theme: technology has become the form of truth and therefore has come to transform the university. For example, Jean-François Lyotard defined techno-science as where "technology plays the role of furnishing the proof of scientific arguments: it allows one to say of a scientific utterance that claim to be true, 'here is a case of it'." ("New Technologies," included in *Political Writings*, translated by Bill Readings and Kevin Paul Geiman (Minneapolis: University of Minnesota Press, 1993) page 15.) Lyotard describes the new technologies emergent in our time as technologies of language with the following characteristics: (1) increased exterioriza-tion of knowledge, (2) an increased role for technology in knowledge production, (3) the spread of automatization, or informatization, in production, and (4) an increase in commodities with integrated automata (p. 16). Jacques Derrida similarly considers the change in the concept of work that underlies the contemporary transformation of the university as "an effect of techno-science, with the worldwide-izing virtualization and delocalization of tele-work" in "The University without Condition" *Without Alibi*, translated by Peggy Kamuf (Stanford: Stanford University Press, 2002) p. 226. The essay by Lyotard was published in 1982, shortly after his well-known 1979 book *The Postmodern Condition: A Report on Knowledge*, translated by Geoff Bennington and Brian Massumi (Minneapolis: University of Minnesota Press, 1984) some of whose main theses it summarizes and extends. The book argued that the two main legitimations of modernity were liberty and science and that they have currently been eclipsed by performativity, a human *doing* or *making*. He makes use of the argument noticed above that science comes under the control of the language game of performativity because of the production of proofs (pp. 46–47) but also claims that "technology became important to contemporary knowledge only through the mediation of a generalized spirit of performativity" (p. 45). The university thus succumbs to the criterion of performativity that is the same criterion operative in the social system as a whole (page 48). Lyotard seems to leave unexplained why the performative spirit came to predominate, though he does derive from Wittgenstein the possibility of a post-modern legitimation not based on performativity (p. 41). Postmodernity, in Lyotard's use of the term, seems to refer both to a regime of performativity and to the possibility of its being supplanted by something else. While there may be an equivocation here, or it may be deliberate, the fixing on performativity as the legitimation of a university thoroughly immersed in socio-technical networks indistinct from the society as a whole strikes a fundamental truth. Whether this should be seen as a liberation from a traditional hierarchy inherent in knowledge or a loss of measure for mere applicability (or even both) is a matter for considerable debate in contemporary philosophy and social theory.

The idea of a network is deeply rooted in the cybernetic model of techno-science. The work of Gilles Deleuze and Félix Guattari has been very influential in the idea of a network that is used in contemporary social theory and the use of network as an emerging utopia is deeply imbedded in their work. It is based in their analysis in *Anti-Oedipus: Capitalism and Schizophrenia*, translated by Robert Hurley, Mark Seem and Helen R. Lane (Minneapolis: University of Minnesota Press, 1983) and other texts of capitalism as a process of deterritorialization and reterritorialization. "Unconscious representation therefore comprises essentially, by virtue of its own *law*, a represented that is displaced in relation to an agency in a constant state of displacement. ...displacement refers to very different movements: at times, the movement through which desiring-production is continually overcoming the limit, becoming deterritorialized, causing its flows to escape, going beyond the threshold of representation; at times, on the contrary, the movement through which the limit itself is displaced, and now passes into the interior of the representation that performs the artificial reterritorializations of desire" (p. 313). The consequence of this analysis is that "one can never go far enough in the direction of deterritorialization: you haven't seen anything yet — an irreversible process." The irreversibility of this process is what generates the observation of "a profoundly

artificial nature in the perverted reterritorializations"
(p. 321). But, before one accepts this account, one should
ask whether reterritorializations are always perverted. It
may not seem so at first, given their emphasis on the "proliferation" and "multiplication" of deterritorializations
(see also Gilles Deleuze and Félix Guattari, *A Thousand
Plateaus: Capitalism and Schizophrenia*, translated by Brian
Massumi (London: The Athlone Press, 1988) *passim*,
eg. 183). But for Deleuze and Guattari such prolifera-
tions are written upon the primary deterritorialization
that they complicate and reproduce but never undo. The
consequence of this phrasing is that all defences of place
or locality are understood in terms of a reterritorialization
that cannot destructure, or even really influence, the primary deterritorialization. Since "reterritorialization must
not be confused with a return to a primitive or older territoriality; it necessarily implies a set of artifices by which
one element, itself deterritorialized, serves as a new territoriality for another, which has lost its territoriality as
well" (*A Thousand Plateaus: Capitalism and Schizophrenia*,
p. 174). Any politics of place is figured as attempting
perversely to reverse a deterritorialization that it, in principle, cannot reverse. Continued attempts to defend and
extend a prior border that inscribed a limit to expansion
and proliferation so that a different politico-cultural project could emerge cannot be captured by this vocabulary.

Thus, Deleuze and Guattari's analysis leads them to cast all attempts at localizations within the deterritorialized system as artificial and perverted since they do not stand outside the system but are reactions generated by the process of deterritorialization itself. Despite the apparently esoteric nature of this critique of Deleuze and Guattari, it is important for the analysis of the crucial role of social movements as (non-perverted) localizations.

The notion of a network thus introduces a crucial division into contemporary philosophy and social theory that still requires further thought: is the network a utopia of non-hierarchical relations or is it a loss of measure, and thus enlightenment, by subsuming reflection entirely within the social order? It is impossible to attempt to address such a question here, but let me make the following point. It is commonplace to assume nowadays that any sort of border or boundary, which defines a limit to expansion or movement, must be an arbitrary exercise of power that is to be resisted and overcome. Bill Readings (in *The University in Ruins*, pp. 96–98) has noticed this prevalent assumption also, though he limits its effectivity to "cultural studies" and provides neither an account of why it is prevalent nor a critique. I have criticized this assumption in an article on Michael Hardt and Antonio Negri's influential book *Empire* (Cambridge: Harvard University Press, 2000), which is based on Deleuze and Guattari's theory, called "Empire, Borders, Place: A Critique of Hardt and Negri's Concept of Empire" *Theory and Event*, Vol. 7, No. 3, 2004 which is available at <http://muse.jhu. edu/journals.theory_and_event/v007/7.3angus.html>.

Hardt and Negri have argued that "the local moment or perspective gives priority to the reterritorializing barriers or boundaries and the global moment privileges the mobility of deterritorializing flows" (p. 45) and that "in its deterritorialized autonomy ... this biopolitical existence of the multitude has the potential to be transformed into an autonomous mass of intelligent productivity, into an absolute democratic power" (p. 344). Thus, by simply accepting the assumption that crossing borders is always emancipatory, they can never investigate the constitution of an inside-outside relation but resort to a continual rhetoric of "no outside" that pervades the narrative but which cannot formulate the necessity of the outside to the constitution of the inside. This latter task can only be performed through the articulation of a limit, a measure, which requires reference to the concept of enlightenment.

The assumption that transgressing borders is always emancipatory is dangerous because it leads one to the further assumption that a network, and network society, is an egalitarian overcoming of hierarchy. If it is also a loss of measure, the network involves an abandonment of enlightenment. Understanding the network society as rooted in techno-science allows one to ask the underlying question: through what "mode of appearance" does the world appear in the network? Addressing this question would allow one to work out a perspective on the network that is not a simple logic of progress or decline but fixes on the transformations taking place in order to describe the possibility of a renovated project of enlightenment. This is what I have attempted to do in my analysis of the university in the text.

REFERENCES AND FURTHER READING

CHAPTER ONE: WHAT IS THE UNIVERSITY?

The statistics at the beginning of this chapter are taken from the introduction to James E. Côté and Anton L. Allahar, *Ivory Tower Blues: A University System in Crisis* (Toronto: University of Toronto Press, 2007). This book gives a good description of the current state of affairs in contemporary universities from the viewpoints of the major participants. Their conclusion that education and training are distinct but could be synthesized in higher education, that "liberal education and vocational training do not have to be competing missions" (p. 185), and that "liberal arts is about the dissemination of knowledge and the preparation of well-rounded citizens," makes it a well-informed defence of what I will discuss as the "public university" in Chapter 3. Many Canadian academics are still deeply committed to this ideal of the university, especially given its evident superiority to the corporate university that has replaced it. The issue, however, which I address in the main text, is what forces have led to this decay. The previous situation cannot be simply reinstated without addressing the causes of the decay. I don't spend much time in this book in criticizing commonplaces concerning the university, but it is important to cut through such illusions to get to the core of the contemporary issue. See in this connection the excellent critique of the notions of an "ivory tower" and a "community of scholars" by L.M. Findlay in "Realizing Community: The University as Community" which is included in L.M. and Isobel Findlay (eds.), *Realizing Community: Multidisciplinary Perspectives* (Saskatoon: University of Saskatchewan, 1995).

CHAPTER TWO: EDUCATION AS ENLIGHTENMENT

The edition of Rilke that I used is Rainer Maria Rilke, *Letters to a Young Poet*, translated by M.D. Herter Norton (Norton and Co.: New York, 1993). I have indicated quotations from this source within the main text with a page number that refers to this edition. The quote from Kant in the text is from the essay "What is Enlightenment?" It is included in the collection *On History*, translated by Lewis White Beck (Indianapolis: Bobbs-Merrill, Library of Liberal Arts, 1963) p. 5.

CHAPTER THREE: THE UNIVERSITY IN HISTORY

One of the "conservative critiques" that I have in mind is that by Peter C. Emberley and Waller R. Newell, *Bankrupt Education: The Decline of Liberal Education in Canada* (Toronto: University of Toronto Press, 1994). There is a lot of informed analysis in the book, especially the important historical argument that "Canadian education theory and practice had evolved their own rich application of the universal standards of liberal learning to suit our country's specific circumstances, a unique hybrid of Anglo-European influences including Hegelianism and Scottish common-sense philosophy" (p. 11). Neither are they wrong about the empty-headed reformism that has driven many recent educational changes. However, they fail to focus on any structural or basic reasons behind these changes and thereby fall into blaming "neo-Marxist theory" (p. 11) and "the ideology of systemic victimization" (p. 59) for the current situation and advocating a return to the past. Such rhetorics of a past golden age are pervasive these days since professors really can remember better days in the university. But an analysis is not complete until it is understood *why* those better days have gone. Frank Donoghue, *The Last Professors: The Corporate University and the Fate of the Humanities* (New York: Fordham University Press, 2008) is much better at analysis, explaining well why "prestige" has become the recent guarantor for university success,

charting the history of business attacks on liberal education, and therefore is much more realistic in calling for
humanists to challenge the corporate model by keeping
"its most precious tenets from becoming articles of faith
for everyone: students, society at large, even disempowered
humanists" (p. 136) through "a thorough familiarity with
how the university works" (p. 137). My intentions in this
book are not far from the tasks that Donoghue outlines in
his concluding chapter.

On Humboldt and the University of Berlin see Paul
R. Sweet, *Wilhelm von Humboldt: A Biography* (Columbus:
Ohio State University Press, 1980). A good selection of
Humboldt's writings in English can be found in *Humanist
Without Portfolio: An Anthology of the Writings of Wilhelm
von Humboldt*, translated by Marianne Cowan (Detroit:
Wayne State University Press, 1963). The two quotes from
Humboldt in the text can be found on pages 125 and
103. The story of the University of London is told in the
useful survey article by Alison Hearn "Interdisciplinarity/
Extradisciplinarity: On the University and the Active
Pursuit of Community" in *History of Intellectual Culture*,
Vol. 3, No. 1, 2003.

German philosopher Jürgen Habermas wrote two
important articles that intervened in the debates about
the German university in the 1960s. "The University in
a Democracy—Democratization of the University" was

given as a lecture at the University of Berlin in January 1967 and is included in Jürgen Habermas, *Toward a Rational Society*, translated by Jeremy J. Shapiro (Boston: Beacon Press, 1970). Habermas begins from the realistic notion that "universities must transmit technically exploitable knowledge" (p. 1) and then tries to add public functions to this starting point by arguing that the sciences still require reflexive critical inquiry in a form that connects them to the discussion of political alternatives that characterizes the humanities. His "The Idea of the University—Learning Processes," was translated in *New German Critique*, Vol. 41, No. 3, 1987. It usefully reviews the history of German Idealism, not only Humboldt, in its intrinsic connection to the idea of the university as the unity of teaching and research. Habermas describes its basic notion as "a notion of philosophy which proceeds from the self-reference of the knowing subject and develops all substantive knowledge along the path of a reflexive movement of thought [which] could simultaneously satisfy both specialist's esoteric interest in science and the layman's exoteric interest in self-understanding and enlightenment" (p. 11). He argues in a manner identical to the previously mentioned article that, though this idea of the university is no longer viable (pp. 18, 20), it is "the communicative or discursive forms of scientific argumentation which in the final analysis hold the learning processes together in their various functions" (p. 21). In his view these communicative processes are inherent in research throughout university disciplines and can provide the basis for a renewal of democratic processes in the university. The perspective that I develop can accept this influence where it occurs, but is less confident that this classical ideal of rational equality is pervasive in contemporary corporate-funded research or that the concept of critique that may be required in scientific inquiry meets the ideal in humanistic studies that is based on the philosophical concept of enlightenment. In particular, I argue that a relation to the lived world of non-specialists is essential for the university to regain its ideal of enlightenment.

A good current edition of Newman is John Henry Newman, *The Idea of a University* (Notre Dame: University of Notre Dame Press, 2007). The quote from Newman in the text is from page 115 of this edition; the phrase "true culture" is on page 115. The importance of Newman for English-language discussions of the idea of the university is illustrated by the extent to which it remains an explicit reference for contemporary writers who often conclude that they can do no better than endorse Newman's conception. See, for two examples of this sort, J. M. Cameron, *On the Idea of the University* (Toronto: University of Toronto Press, 1978) and Jaroslav Pelikan, *The Idea of the University: A Reexamination* (New Haven:

Yale University Press, 1992). A good contemporary edition of Arnold is Matthew Arnold, *Culture and Anarchy and other writings*, edited by Sefan Collini (Cambridge: Cambridge University Press, 2006, originally 1867–69). Arnold's definitions and views of culture are throughout the book but most evident in the first chapter. The references to civilization and machinery are on page 63 and the quoted text is from page 65. The references to the relation between science and culture are on page 60. The statement about the transition from religion to culture in Canadian university studies is based on A.B. McKillop in *Matters of Mind: The University in Ontario, 1791–1951* (Toronto: University of Toronto Press, 1994) pp. 219–231. Immanuel Kant's words can be found in *The Conflict of the Faculties*, translated by Mary J. Gregor (Lincoln: University of Nebraska, 1979) p. 55. The quoted statement on the nature of Canadian universities is from Glen A. Jones, "The Idea of a Canadian University" in *Interchange*, Vol. 29, No. 1, p. 78.

T.H. Huxley's ideas on liberal education can be found in "A Liberal Education; and Where to Find It." Huxley's remarks on Scottish and English universities are in "Universities: Actual and Ideal." The Johns Hopkins lecture is entitled "Address on University Education." All these addresses are available in *T.H. Huxley on Education* (Cambridge: Cambridge University Press, 1971). The quotation in the text is from the first of these on page 91. His preference for German universities is evident on page 95 and his view that a liberal education in literature, languages and history should eventually be adopted at the South London Working-Men's College is expressed on pages 97–98. To the extent that Huxley attempted to knit together practicality and a liberal education, we may well see him as one of our most important predecessors.

I have based my references to the multiversity on statements by Clark Kerr, President of the University of California, and Claude Bissell, President of the University of Toronto, not only because they were two of the most eloquent expositors of the new "realistic" trend but because their views had considerable influence in both political and university circles at the time. The first two quotes are from Clark Kerr, *The Uses of the University* (Cambridge: Harvard, 1964) on pages 41 and 124. The third quote is from Claude Bissell, *The Strength of the University* (Toronto: University of Toronto Press, 1968) from page 56. References to "adapting" occur throughout the texts in question, of course, but note specifically page 124 of Kerr and page 233 of Bissell. In the 1960s the conception of the multiversity as serving the powerful in society was opposed by the student movement, which renamed it the "knowledge factory" and proceeded to search for and advocate another relation of the university to society. One such proposal was "the critical university." I have decided to discuss neither the student movement nor the political conflicts of 1960s universities here not only because it threatens to become a large historical theme, but also because I do not want to suggest that the important struggles of the 1960s can be simply resurrected today. The university has gone a lot further down the road that opened up then and we must take our departure from our present situation, even while we may remain faithful at a different level to the struggles of the past.

CHAPTER FOUR: THE CORPORATE UNIVERSITY

On the new for-profit, private universities, see Richard S. Ruch, *Higher Ed, Inc.: The Rise of the For-Profit University* (Baltimore: Johns Hopkins University Press, 2001). George Keller claims in his Foreword on page x that there are more such for-profit higher education institutions in the United States than there are non-profit ones. Chapter 3 gives an outline of the history of this development.

Bill Readings' *The University in Ruins* (Cambridge: Harvard University Press, 1996) has been widely discussed. Its original thesis is that the university has lost its role in articulating the culture of the nation-state and no longer has any referent. Thus, the contentless rhetoric of excellence appears and begins to dominate the university. It is an important argument. In my view, however,

the rhetoric of excellence may come and go as rhetorics tend to do. For Readings, its importance is rooted in
the idea of a lack of reference, though I think that many
other rhetorics could cover a similar failing. More important, Readings' notion that the university has no referent
is over-determined by his reliance on semiotic analysis. I
can't find any other content to the idea of "no referent"
than the fact that the university no longer serves as legitimation within the national economy, in which case it is no
more or less referentless than any other enterprise—for
which I use the term public-private enterprise. In fact,
Frank Donoghue's idea (mentioned in the references to
the previous chapter) that prestige has become the goal of
universities in a competitive market gives greater content
to Readings' discussion. In addition to his book *The Last
Professors* mentioned above, Donoghue pointed out in an
article called "Prestige" in *Profession 2006* that "But the
new sponsor, prestige, is dangerously nonreferential, eerily
similar to "excellence," which Bill Readings critiqued in
The University in Ruins. Prestige is a dimension of a college's public relations rather than its day-to-day practices;
it is the province of development officers and enrollment
managers, not professors" (p. 157). The reference of a
shoe-making enterprise is shoes, and the fashion market
for shoes, and the reference of a university is credentials,
and the competitive market for credentials. I think that

these two errors account for the fact that Readings' book rambles inconclusively to an end even though his analysis of the contentless nature of excellence is important.

The distinction between use value and exchange value is grounded in classical economics and was used by Marx to analyze the process of labour under capitalism. More recently, it has been applied to women's work outside the paid economy and to environmental "uses" such as clean air, wild animals, etc., which do not have a price. Both of these applications centre on the difficulty within a capitalist society of rendering value to any thing or being that does not have a price. My article "Subsistence as a Social Right: A New Political Ideal for Socialism?" published in *Studies in Political Economy*, No. 65, Summer 2001, is one version of an environmentalist use of the distinction.

My description of the effects of the consumer model on the university is based on my observation of the phenomenon over the last several decades. There are a number of recent books on the corporatization of the university. The situation in the United States, being more advanced in this direction than that in Canada, has produced quite a few. See, for example, Jennifer Washburn, *University Inc.: The Corporate Corruption of Higher Education* (New York: Basic Books, 2005); Henry Giroux, *The University in Chains* (Boulder: Paradigm Publishers, 2007); Stanley Aronowitz, *The Knowledge Factory: Dismantling the*

Corporate University and Creating True Higher Learning (Boston: Beacon Press, 2000) and Geoffry D. White (ed.), *Campus, Inc.: Corporate Power in the Ivory Tower* (New York: Prometheus Books, 2000). The Canadian situation has been monitored very effectively by Janice Newson and her collaborators in publications such as Janice Newson and Howard Buchbinder, *The University Means Business* (Toronto: Garamond Press, 1988); Jan Currie and Janice Newson (eds.), *Universities and Globalization: Critical Perspectives* (Thousand Oaks: Sage, 1998) and Janice Newson, "The Corporate-Linked University: From Social Project to Market Force" in *Canadian Journal of Communication*, Vol. 23, No. 1, Winter 1988.

Regarding the expectation of a B for mere participation in a course, see the recent widely circulated *New York Times* article by Max Roosevelt, "Student Expectations Seen as Causing Grade Disputes" in *The New York Times*, 17 February 2009. This article was reprinted in *The Globe and Mail* soon after under the heading "I attended the lecture — that should earn me an automatic B." A similar article on the expectation of a B, referring to research on the matter by Ellen Greenberger of the University of California, Irvine, entitled "Pass me, I tried hard, students say," was distributed by Canwest News Service in April 2009 and was likely reprinted in many Canadian newspapers. It should be noticed that evidence for this phenomenon originates in the United States. While there is certainly anecdotal evidence of a pressure in the same direction in Canada, it is not yet clear whether the situation is as dismal. Figures for the percentage composition of university teaching by part-time, sessional and contract faculty are taken from Lykke de la Cour, "The Casualization of Academic Labour at York University" which is available at <www.yorkdemocraticforum.org/node/23> through the York Democratic Forum, which is a very good source for current information on university politics. Figures vary somewhat due to the way in which various job categories are counted, but these figures are representative of most estimates and are telling of a general trend. The announcement by the Presidents of McGill University, Université de Montréal, University of Toronto, University of British Columbia, and University of Alberta that they would promote the policy of elite research universities was made in "Our Universities Can be Smarter" in *Maclean's*, 3 August 2009.

CHAPTER FIVE: KNOWLEDGE AS A COMMODITY

Information about the Public Knowledge Project is available at <http://pkp.sfu.ca/>. It describes itself in the following way: "The Public Knowledge Project is dedicated to improving the scholarly and public quality of research. It operates through a partnership among the Faculty of

Education at the University of British Columbia, the Simon Fraser University Library, the School of Education at Stanford University, and the Canadian Centre for Studies in Publishing at Simon Fraser University. The partnership brings together faculty members, librarians, and graduate students dedicated to exploring whether and how new technologies can be used to improve the professional and public value of scholarly research. Its research program is investigating the social, economic, and technical issues entailed in the use of online infrastructure and knowledge management strategies to improve both the scholarly quality and public accessibility and coherence of this body of knowledge in a sustainable and globally accessible form. It continues to be an active player in the open access movement, as it provides the leading open source software for journal and conference management and publishing."

My involvement in issues of academic freedom has been, until recently, only through daily university politics. The motivation for trying to think more systematically about it derives from the recent controversy over administrative violation of academic freedom in the proposed hiring of David Noble by the Department of Humanities at Simon Fraser University (SFU). Documents relevant to this controversy can be found at <www.ianangus.ca> and the Canadian Association of University Teachers (CAUT) inquiry can be found on their web site at <www.caut.ca> in the section on academic freedom. The final court settlement after Noble sued SFU resulted, characteristically, in the SFU administration paying an undisclosed amount of public money to Noble and an agreement that Noble would not speak about the conditions of the settlement. For background on academic freedom see the excellent history by Michiel Horn, *Academic Freedom in Canada: A History* (Toronto: University of Toronto Press, 1999). The CAUT-ACPPU, Policy Statement on Academic Freedom (approved by the CAUT Council, May 1977) can be read at <www.caut.ca/pages.asp?page=247&lang=1>.

One scholar who has used his perception of the "de-institutionalization of knowledge" and the "change in the location of knowledge production" to ground a far-reaching reflection that "the disabling factor in intellectual work is not the external threats to academic freedom but the internal compliance with the social agenda" is Jerry Zaslove, "The 'Lost Utopia' of Academic Freedom" in L.M. Findlay and Paul M. Bidwell (eds.), *Pursuing Academic Freedom* (Saskatoon: Purich Publishing, 2001) pages 152 and 165.

The Manitoba initiative was announced by the NDP government in the annual Crown speech in 2006. Its current form can be viewed at <www.manitoba.ca/tuition-rebate/index.html> where it is stated that "You are entitled to receive a 60% income tax rebate on your eligible tuition fees to a maximum of $25,000. You can claim your rebate over as little as six years or as long as twenty years." The tuition rebate was based on the New Brunswick model. See the CBC news report available at <www.cbc.ca/canada/manitoba/story/2006/11/15/throne-speech.html> and the story by Tessa Vanderhart in *The Manitoban* (the student newspaper at the University of Manitoba) that was widely reprinted in the student press. One reprint is available at <www.peak.sfu.ca/the-peak/2006-3/issue13/ne-toba.html>.

CHAPTER SIX: TRANSFORMATION OF KNOWLEDGE
The quoted UNESCO statement is by Marco Antonio Rodrigues Dias, Director of the Division of Higher Education of UNESCO in his Foreward to Alfonso Borrero Cabal, *The University as an Institution Today: Topics for Reflection* (UNESCO, 1993) which is available at <www.idrc.ca/openebooks/438-7/#page_2>.

For a thorough discussion of the impact of new forms of knowledge production on the university one can fruitfully begin with the article by Gerard Delanty called "The Idea Of The University In The Global Era: From Knowledge As An End To The End Of Knowledge?" that appeared in the journal *Social Epistemology*, Vol. 12, No. 1, 1988. The whole journal issue is given over to this article, critical responses, and a reply by Delanty. He argues that "The producer and recipient of knowledge is no longer the scholar and student engaged in scholarly discourse in the tutorial. Knowledge is being de-personalized, deterritorialized andglobalized. It is being taken out of its traditional context and disseminated by newmedia of communication" (p. 19).

French philosopher Jacques Derrida engaged in several significant reflections on the current transformation of the university provoked by globalization, or *mondialisation*, and informatization. He proposed in "The Principle of Reason: The University in the Eyes of its Pupils" included in *Eyes of the University* (Stanford: Stanford University Press, 2004) for the university a future in which "the responsibility of a community of thinking for which the border between basic and end-oriented research would no longer be secured, or in any event not under the same conditions as before" even though he thinks that "it is not certain that such thinking can bring together a community or found an institution in the traditional sense of these words" (p. 148). In his reflections on Kant's view of the university, Derrida claimed that the line between inside and outside the university, which was a distinction already problematic for Kant to draw, is impossible to sustain in our own time. In "Mochlos, or The Conflict of Faculties" — which is also included in *Eyes of the University*— he pointedly asked "where does a publication begin?" and condensed the contemporary transformation into the observation that "once the library is no longer the ideal type of the archive, the university no longer remains the center of knowledge and can no longer provide its subjects with a representation of that center" (pp. 99, 94). I think that Derrida is right to connect the destiny of the university to the inside/outside distinction and to think this through the spatio-temporal changes involved in globalization and correlative shifts in the dominant media of communication. I have used his crystallizing focus on this change through the loss of the library as archive in the text, though I have developed it independently.

The idea that communication studies is a study of the spatio-temporal changes induced by various media of communication, including their complex interplay, was pioneered by Harold Innis in *Empire and Communications* (Toronto: University of Toronto Press, 1972), *The Bias of Communication* (Toronto: University of Toronto Press, 1951), and *Changing Concepts of Time* (Toronto: University of Toronto Press, 1952). The work of Marshall McLuhan built upon this foundation, influenced Jean Baudrillard, and is therefore responsible for both the insight and exaggeration around the term "postmodernism." A good summary account of the changes brought about by the Internet is provided in Mark Poster, *What's the Matter with the Internet?* (Minneapolis: University of

Minnesota Press, 2001) which builds upon his earlier *The Mode of Information* (Chicago: University of Chicago Press, 1990). Poster's work is in general a good account of what has been said on these matters by recent French philosophers and a reliable guide to the wider literature. The account of information in the text supplements the previous account in Chapter 7 of Ian Angus, *Primal Scenes of Communication: Communication, Consumerism, Social Movements* (Albany: State University of New York Press, 2000).

The impact of techno-science on society has given rise to many social scientific accounts since knowledge has always been important to modern societies and accounts for the founding of research-teaching universities. The notion of a "risk society" arose in the 1980s to describe a society in which continuous industrial use of techno-logical innovations has led to incalculable consequences such that the distinction between calculable risks and incalculable threats is violated. See Ulrich Beck, *Ecological Enlightenment: On the Politics of the Risk Society*, trans-lated by Mark A. Ritter (New Jersey: Humanities Press, 1995). William Leiss coined the related term "risk com-munication" to refer to the social and legal process of communicating risks both prior to decision making and in reckoning responsibility for consequences. See his web site at <www.leiss.ca> for many materials and papers.

Risk society is thus a self-reflexive form of modern society that takes modern industrial use of technology as an object of reflection. However, proponents of the notion of "risk society," are haunted by a technocratic element, which implies that these risks are manageable by sufficiently enlightened experts. For this reason, the concept of techno-science is more productive in that it raises the issue, not only of the institutionalization of science, but also of the social transformations brought about by technology and those which might change its social role.

Studies of the impact of computer technology and informatics on the economy are now legion. The quote in the text is from page 60 of the influential early study by Jeremy Rifkin, *The End of Work* (New York: G.P. Putnam's Sons, 1995). The idea of network society also refers to the informational, or computational, form of such technological innovation. For a comprehensive account, see Manuel Castells, *The Information Age: Economy, Society and Culture, Vol. 1: The Rise of the Network Society* (Oxford: Blackwell, 2000). The quotes are from pages 75–76 and 70. The five characteristics of network society are from the section entitled "The Information Technology Paradigm" on pages 69–76.

The emergence of social movements over crises of identity in the network society has been the subject of a great deal of thinking and research in the humanities and social sciences over the last three decades. It is simply not possible to summarize that literature here. The account in the text is based primarily on my own work on this question. An accessible starting point is the previous short book that I published in the Semaphore series called *Emergent Publics: An Essay on Social Movements and Democracy* (Winnipeg: Arbeiter Ring, 2001). See also *Primal Scenes of Communication: Communication, Consumerism, Social Movements* (Albany: State University of New York Press, 2000) and the more recent *Identity and Justice* (Toronto: University of Toronto Press, 2008). A model of an opposition between network society and social movements is also proposed by Manuel Castells in *The Information Age: Economy, Society and Culture, Vol. 2: The Power of Identity* (Oxford: Blackwell, 2004). He argues that "the dominant logic of the network society triggers its own challenges, in the form of communal resistance identities, and of project identities potentially emerging from these spaces, *under conditions and through processes that are specific to each institutional and cultural context*" (p. 424). While at times Castells seems to get caught in the unproductive sociological dilemma of whether such movements are necessary or not (see, for example, p. 420), my attempt is to illuminate the point of emergence of such movements and explore their logic. Castells' work, on the other hand, is full of useful sociological descriptions and detail.

CHAPTER SEVEN: WHAT IS POSSIBLE?
One important recent book that collects various attempts to reform the university under contemporary conditions is Mark Côté, Richard J.F. Day and Greig de Peuter (eds.), *Utopian Pedagogy: Radical Experiments Against Neoliberal Globalization* (Toronto: University of Toronto Press, 2007).

I have addressed the question of how to design a unity of knowledge in contemporary conditions in more detail in an article entitled "The Telos of the Good Life: Reflections on Interdisciplinarity and Models of Knowledge" in Raphael Foshay (ed.), *The Scope of Interdisciplinarity* (Athabasca University Press, forthcoming).